Conservation Heroes

AL GORE

Conservation Heroes

Ansel Adams

John James Audubon

Rachel Carson

Jacques Cousteau

Jane Goodall

Al Gore

Steve and Bindi Irwin

Chico Mendes

John Muir

Theodore Roosevelt

Conservation Heroes

AL GORE

Tracey Baptiste

CHELSEA HOUSE
An Infobase Learning Company

Chelsea House
An imprint of Infobase Learning
132 West 31st Street
New York, NY 10001

Library of Congress Cataloging-in-Publication Data
Baptiste, Tracey.
  Al Gore / Tracey Baptiste.
    p. cm. — (Conservation heroes)
  Includes bibliographical references and index.
  ISBN 978-1-60413-949-5 (hardcover)
  1. Gore, Albert, 1948-—Juvenile literature. 2. Environmentalists—United States—Biography—Juvenile literature. 3. Nobel Prize winners—United State—Biography—Juvenile literature. 4. United States. Congress. Senate—Biography—Juvenile literature. 5. Vice-Presidents—United States—Biography—Juvenile literature. 6. Vice-Presidential candidates—United States—Biography—Juvenile literature. I. Title. II. Series.
  GE56.G67B37 2010
  333.72092—dc22
  [B]   2010030592

Chelsea House books are available at special discounts when purchased in bulk quantities for businesses, associations, institutions, or sales promotions. Please call our Special Sales Department in New York at (212) 967-8800 or (800) 322-8755.

You can find Chelsea House on the World Wide Web
at http://www.chelseahouse.com.

Text design by: Annie O'Donnell
Cover design by: Takeshi Takahashi
Composition by: Newgen North America
Cover printed by: Bang Printing, Brainerd, MN
Book printed and bound by: Bang Printing, Brainerd, MN
Date printed: March 2011

Printed in the United States of America

10 9 8 7 6 5 4 3 2 1

This book is printed on acid-free paper.

All links and Web addresses were checked and verified to be correct at the time of publication. Because of the dynamic nature of the Web, some addresses and links may have changed since publication and may no longer be valid.

0 3/3 7   0 3 9 6

Contents

Gore's Winning Message

AN IMPORTANT PRIZE

On December 10, 2007, former vice president Al Gore stepped up to a podium to address a gathering of scientists and dignitaries. It was a cold night in Oslo, Norway, and he had an important message. "We, the human species, are confronting a planetary emergency," he said to those in attendance. "But there is hopeful news as well: we have the ability to solve this crisis and avoid the worst—though not all—of its consequences, if we act boldly, decisively, and quickly."

Gore was addressing a gathering of people who had come to listen to his Nobel Peace Prize acceptance speech. He had been awarded the Nobel Peace Prize that year, along with a group of United Nations (UN) scientists, called the UN's Intergovernmental Panel on Climate Change (IPCC), which was formed to find out if Earth was warming and if human activity was a cause in climate change. The Nobel Peace Prize has been given every year since 1901 to people who have worked for peace. In 2007, the Nobel Committee felt that Al Gore and the UN's IPCC scientists were

Al Gore (*center*) and the chairman of the intergovernmental Panel on Climate Change, Dr. Rajendra K. Pachauri (*right*), receive their medals and diplomas at the Nobel Peace Prize ceremony in Oslo, Norway, on December 10, 2007.

working for world peace by bringing the message that people were indeed the cause of global climate change to the world and also by suggesting what people could do to stop their influence on climate change. The committee said that Gore was "the single individual who has done most to create a greater worldwide understanding of the measures that need to be adopted."

Al Gore had worked long and hard to inform people about the effects of climate change on the planet, but he had been working for a long time before that to serve the people of the United States as a politician in the House of Representatives, the Senate, and the White House. Gore's greatest career disappointment came in 2000, when he lost the election to be president of the United States. He noted in his Nobel Peace Prize speech that almost exactly seven years before that night, he had lost the presidential election, but out of it had come a new way to continue serving people just as he had done throughout his political career.

Following the election, Gore began to do speaking engagements and chose the subject of global warming as his main topic. It was one that was very familiar to him. While growing up, he had had many influences that led to his observations that Earth needed more care than people were giving it. One of his college professors started measuring warming trends on the planet over the course of several years. When Gore read a book called *Silent Spring*—Rachel Carson's book about the adverse effects of putting harmful toxins

THE NOBEL PEACE PRIZE AND THE WHITE HOUSE

Al Gore is not the only White House occupant to win a Nobel Peace Prize. Former President Jimmy Carter became a Nobel Laureate in 2002. The Nobel Committee cited his "untiring effort to find peaceful solutions to international conflicts, to advance democracy and human rights, and to promote economic and social development." Carter was awarded the prize at the same time that President George W. Bush was authorized by the U.S. House and Senate to begin military action in Iraq. The head of the Nobel Committee, Gunnar Berge, acknowledged that giving the prize to Carter was partly a criticism of the way the United States was handling the conflict with Iraq.

In 2009, the Nobel Committee honored sitting President Barack Obama during his first year in office. The committee chose Obama for the prize "for his extraordinary efforts to strengthen international diplomacy and cooperation between peoples." The committee also wanted to encourage "Obama's vision of and work for a world without nuclear weapons."

into the environment—it was not a difficult jump for him to take on what he called a "planetary crisis."

Like Gore, the scientists who were on the UN's IPCC panel were honored by the Nobel Committee "for their efforts to build up and disseminate greater knowledge about manmade climate change, and to lay the foundations for the measures that are needed to counteract such change." They, too, understood that the need to arrest the human impact on global warming was great; therefore, these scientists, who were from several different countries, worked together to conduct studies and publish their findings so that governments could use the data to make changes that could counteract the problem. Although Gore and the head of the IPCC panel both received a diploma and gold medal from the Nobel Committee that night in Oslo, they all knew that their work was far from over. Many people still do not believe that climate change is happening, or that its cause is manmade despite the many studies supporting these theories and the thousands of scientists who have agreed with the findings of those studies. Educating people about climate change was still the main goal of Gore and those scientists.

WHAT IS GLOBAL WARMING?

"Global warming may not seem like one of our biggest dangers, but it is," Al Gore wrote in his 2006 book *An Inconvenient Truth: The Crisis of Global Warming*. The problem is that Earth's atmosphere is being filled by large amounts of greenhouse gases. Greenhouse gases are gases in our atmosphere that hold in heat. They include carbon dioxide (CO_2), methane, and nitrous oxide. In preindustrial times, the amount of greenhouse gases in the world was enough to trap some of the sun's heat and to let more escape. It was a good balance. However, since the burning of fossil fuels, such as oil, natural gas, and coal, that are used in cars, homes, factories, and power plants has increased significantly in the last 200 years, the amount of greenhouse gases in the atmosphere has increased. Now, not as

A polar bear climbs on melting ice in Franz Josef Land, an archipelago in the Arctic Ocean, far north of Russia. Warmer temperatures make it more difficult for animals to find food.

much of the Sun's heat escapes into space—most of it stays in our atmosphere. The retention is slowly heating up the planet. This is what global warming is about.

The evidence to support global warming is so dramatic that it can be observed by anyone. The clearest evidence can be seen in the disappearance of glaciers all over the planet. Glaciers are huge masses of compacted ice, thousands of years old, which flow slowly over land. Glaciers are miles long and miles wide and can be up to two stories tall. It would take a tremendous amount of heat to melt all of that ice. However, glaciers that existed just a few decades ago are now gone. In *An Inconvenient Truth,* Gore shows comparison photos of glaciers that have disappeared. He shows a 1932 picture of Boulder Glacier in Glacier National Park, Montana, where the packed mound of ice sits heavily over the land. In a 1988 photo, the glacier is no longer there. The Rhone Glacier in Switzerland travelled near a snow-capped mountain in 1906. In 2003, the glacier is gone, and the snow-capped mountain is now covered with greenery. In Patagonia, Argentina, the Upsala Glacier was once a magnificent stretch of ice. By 2004, it had become a lake.

In addition to the easy-to-observe evidence, scientists have done many studies to document how global warming is taking place, when it began, and what the cause is. They study glaciers because the ice in glaciers contains hundreds of years of information about the planet's atmosphere. An ice core—a length of ice cut down through the center of a glacier—gives information about every year that the glacier has been in existence. Scientists can read this

THE MEDIA AND GLOBAL WARMING

Dr. Naomi Oreskes at the University of California did an independent study of expert scientific findings about global warming for a period of 10 years. From a random sampling of articles, she found none that disagreed with the main findings: the climate was changing, Earth's atmosphere was getting hotter, and the human factor was the main cause of these changes. She also studied the articles about global warming in four major American newspapers. She found that more than half of the articles cast doubt on the cause of global warming. Dr. Oreskes and her team concluded that the news had falsely given the impression that the scientific community was embroiled in a heated debate about whether or not humans were contributing to global warming. In fact, the scientific community sees the human effect in global warming as a proven fact.

information the way they read tree rings because there are clear lines in the ice that separate every year. The ice core data revealed that over a period of a thousand years, the most dramatic warming has occurred in the last 200 years. Unlike other warm periods in the history of Earth, this warming trend has lasted much longer and is only getting hotter.

Despite the evidence, there are still many who do not believe in global warming and who ridicule Al Gore for his statements. In his 2010 State of the Union Address, President Barack Obama said, "I know that there are those who disagree with the overwhelming scientific evidence on climate change. But here's the thing: Even if you doubt the evidence, providing incentives for energy-efficiency and clean energy are the right thing to do for our future." Gore's goal in addressing climate change due to global warming aims both to prevent harming the planet irrevocably and to find better ways to create energy as the president stated above. He hopes that individuals, businesses, and governments will take the steps necessary to significantly reduce the effects that people have on the climate and the planet. "It is our only home," Gore says in *An Inconvenient Truth*. "And we must take care of it."

Gore's efforts to educate people about climate change due to global warming have fallen on some deaf ears. Yet, for many other people, his message is making a significant impact. Still, Gore continues to work to ensure that solutions are being formulated. This is only one part of a life dedicated to service. Al Gore has been working to better people and the planet almost since his birth.

One Boy, Two Cities

THE FAMILY BUSINESS

"Well, Mr. Gore, Here He Is—On Page 1." That was the headline in the *Nashville Tennessean* on April 1, 1948. The front-page news announced Albert Arnold Gore Jr., son of Senator Albert Gore, to the world. Gore had actually arrived the day before, on March 31, 1948. Yet the announcement of his birth had been plotted by his father for months. Albert Sr.'s friendly political rivalry with Tennessee House of Representatives congressman Estes Kefauver prompted Albert Sr. to call the *Nashville Tennessean* after news of Kefauver's baby girl appeared on an inside page of the newspaper. The elder Gore told his contacts at the paper to ensure that news of his child's birth would get even better press. "If I have a boy baby, I don't want the news buried in the inside of the paper. I want it on page 1 where it belongs," he said. Young Al Gore's life, even before his birth, was always colored by the politics of his father. His involvement in politics was inevitable, as it was the family business.

Albert Sr. was born and raised in Tennessee. His father, Allen Gore, had been a farmer most of his life, and Albert Sr. also owned farms even though he spent most of his adult life in politics. From a young age, Albert Sr. was known to like the limelight. When they were working the farm, sometimes his father, Allen, would look around and find him standing on a tree stump, talking to an imaginary audience. Albert Sr. seemed determined to get away from the farming lifestyle in order to chase bigger dreams. He would go to listen to Cordell Hull, a local Tennessee politician, who would sit outside the Smith County Courthouse and talk to the checkers players.

After college, Albert Sr. became a teacher and then was elected Smith County School Superintendent. Albert Sr. then went on to manage two unsuccessful campaigns by Gordon Browning for the U.S. Senate. But when Browning finally won an election to become governor of Tennessee in 1936, he appointed Albert Sr. Commissioner of Labor. It was his first real job in politics. The year was a busy one for Albert Sr. In 1936, he was completing law school at Nashville YMCA Law School and dating his future wife, Pauline LaFon.

Pauline LaFon was also attending law school. On her father's advice, she attended Vanderbilt University Law School, and became the second female student in the school's history. Pauline was a native Tennessean as well, but she never felt restricted by the limitations that were put on women's education in the 1930s. Fortunately, neither did her father. Pauline was one of three girls in her family, all of whom went to college. Of the options available to her, Pauline felt that law school suited her best. To save money during law school, she lived at the Nashville YWCA for $2 a week and waited tables at the Andrew Jackson Hotel coffee shop. That was where she and Albert Sr. met. He was a 28-year-old school superintendent, and three nights a week, he would come in to get coffee for the long drive back to his home town of Carthage, Tennessee. The two began to date and were married in 1937. By then, Pauline had already graduated from law school and was practicing law at an office in Texarkana, Arkansas. After the wedding, though, Pauline stopped working in order to support Albert Sr. and his political ambitions as the newly appointed Commissioner of Labor.

Soon after they were married, Albert Sr. and Pauline had a daughter they named Nancy. After trying for years to have another child, along came Al Jr. 10 years after their first baby. For Albert Sr., a son was front-page-worthy news.

Following their marriage on April 17, 1937, Pauline became the kind of wife that supported her husband's career in every way. They lived part of the time in Tennessee, tending the farm, and the other part in Washington, D.C., where Albert Sr. carried out his official duties. After his time as Commissioner of Labor, he set his sights on his own political office and was elected to the House of Representatives in 1938. By winning, he took over the House seat that was once held by his mentor, Cordell Hull. By then, Hull was Secretary of State to President Roosevelt.

Albert Sr. was known for enticing voters, pied-piper-like, with his fiddling during the election campaign. Not all the voters liked his fiddling, and his wife advised him to tone down his playing. Her role in his political career was that of a partner. When he was unable to make appearances and speeches, Pauline would stand in for him, and when they sat around the dinner table to discuss political issues, Albert Sr. was as much influenced by the strong liberal views of his wife as he once was by Cordell Hull.

Albert Sr. and Pauline went to Washington as a team because he knew how intelligent his wife was and he trusted her judgment and great political instincts. In his book *Al Gore Jr.: His Life and Career,* author Hank Hillin reported that a Tennessee reporter once wrote that "Pauline was the brains and Albert was the pretty blond." Pauline's brother Whit agreed that Pauline was an asset to Albert Sr. "Albert had a real good woman that was driving him," he said. "She stayed on his duster." In Gore's eulogy for his father, he said that he learned a lot from the relationship that his parents had with each other. Gore said, "He respected her as an equal, if not more."

To free Pauline for her role as a representative's wife in Washington, the couple hired Mrs. Ocie Bell to care for young Nancy. Mrs. Bell was an African-American woman, and in the 1930s and 1940s, the Deep South, where they lived, was still segregated.

Three-year-old Al Gore Jr. poses with sister Nancy, mother Pauline, and father Albert Sr. after the elder Gore announced his intention to run for the U.S. Senate. Ultimately, he served from 1953 to 1970.

Because the family did extensive travelling for Albert Sr.'s campaigns and work, finding places to stay as an integrated family, since they considered Mrs. Bell to be a part of the family, was difficult. There were times when they would have to travel very far to find a hotel that would accommodate them. Sometimes it meant going in through a back entrance and leaving very early in the morning before the other guests had awakened for breakfast. But for Pauline Gore, the injustice of segregation was one she was willing to bear to show that she, for one, did not support it and to show her young family that race should not play a role in how a person should be treated. Pauline's thinking on race relations raised eyebrows among politicians' wives in Washington when she addressed an African-American woman by the title *Mrs.,* instead of by her first name. Calling an African-American adult by their first name was a common show of disrespect at the time.

After Albert Sr. served for nearly 16 years in the House of Representatives, Pauline encouraged him to reach for higher office. They undertook campaigning against Kenneth D. McKellar for the Senate. McKellar's slogan was "Thinking Feller Vote for McKellar." The signs were posted up on every tree along Tennessee roads. When Pauline saw that, she set Albert Sr. down at the kitchen table with paper and pencil and made a pot of coffee. She told her husband, "We've got to answer that placard." By the next day, they had come up with their own slogan, which they hung up above every one of the McKellar posters: "Think Some More and Vote for Gore." McKellar lost the election, and Gore took his seat as a new senator. That year, his son was four years old.

During Albert Sr.'s career in politics, he championed causes for the average Tennessean, those he had grown up with during his years on his own father's farm. One of his first acts in Congress was to bring the Rural Electrification Program into fruition. Because of Albert Sr.'s involvement, the people of Tennessee felt that President Roosevelt had taken a personal interest in getting electrical service to their homes and farms. But another infrastructure plan, this one far more ambitious than electricity, made Albert Sr. famous.

Albert Sr. studied for and authored the Interstate Highway Act—legislation that proposed the highway system as it exists today. While he began working on it during President Roosevelt's term in office, the bill was not signed, nor did the plan take effect, until the 1950s during the Eisenhower administration.

In addition to setting in motion the plans to build a highway system that would vastly improve communication and travel across the country, Albert Sr. encouraged the government to have talks with China. At the time, China, a communist country, was regarded with scorn and was left out of many United Nations talks, but Gore felt that the country needed to be brought in on conversations because he understood that they were an important country on the world stage. At the time, the notion of talking with China was too outrageous for some conservative voters. That idea, coupled with the fact that Albert Sr. opposed the Vietnam War and believed in ending segregation, eventually brought an end to his political career.

In 1971, after 14 years in the House and 18 years in the Senate, he was defeated by Bill Brock who said that he was "out of touch with the voters of Tennessee" and "too liberal." By the time Albert Sr. left office for good, his son, Al, had just finished his studies at Harvard University. Al Gore was also opposed to the Vietnam War,

INTERSTATE AND INTERNET

The Interstate Highway Act, while written by Albert Gore Sr., was not a one-man campaign. It took several people and a number of years for it to come to fruition. When it was first proposed to President Roosevelt, the finances were simply not there to undertake such a project because the country was still embroiled in World War II. During the Eisenhower administration, several people wanted to see the highway system built in different ways. Senator Gore's way turned out to be the most popular even though he did not have an outline for how to finance the building of 41,000 miles (65,983 kilometers) of roads with the estimated $25 billion cost. In the end, it was a combination of Senator Albert Gore Sr.'s bill along with bills from Representative George H. Fallon and a financing bill from Representative Hale Boggs that sealed the deal.

Work on the highway system began in 1956 and ended 10 years later. It laid the infrastructure for travel and commerce in the United States, very much like the Internet paved the way for electronic commerce and communication in the 1980s. Interestingly, it was Al Gore Jr. who saw the potential for the Internet, which was also called the "information super highway" and heralded it as the wave of the future, much as his father had for the interstate highway system.

but he served as a military officer in Vietnam, and when he returned, his own political career began, just as his father's ended.

GROWING UP IN WASHINGTON, D.C.

"My childhood was spent in two places. I grew up half in the city and half in the country," noted Al Gore in his book, *An Inconvenient Truth.* "I'd go from living in a small eighth-floor apartment, whose windows looked out on concrete parking lots and buildings, to a sprawling farm with animals, sunlight, open sky, and the sparkling water of the Caney Fork River."

By the time Al was born to Albert Sr. and Pauline, Albert Sr. was well entrenched in Washington politics. Pauline had long ago given up her career as a lawyer to be her husband's political partner, and Nancy was attending private schools with other Washington politicians' children. Albert Gore Jr. arrived, weighing 9 pounds, 2 ounces (4.1 kilograms), at Columbia Hospital in Washington.

Representative Gore called his office and several colleagues in Washington before making calls to his native Tennessee, including one to the local newspaper. While Albert Sr. was making calls to colleagues, Nancy, then 10 years old, "was at home calling up everybody in the telephone directory" according to the report in the *Nashville Tennessean.*

The idea of calling two places home was going to be one that Al Gore Jr. dealt with for the rest of his life as his parents, though firmly entrenched in politics, insisted on keeping their Tennessee roots very much alive by maintaining their farms there. Albert Sr. had both a cattle farm and a tobacco plantation. While in Washington, the youngest Gore seemed to live a privileged life. He was raised on the top floor of a Washington hotel, The Fairfax, which advertised itself as "Washington's Family Hotel" at the time. The Gores lived rent-free in Suite 809 because a family member owned the hotel. Their neighbors were other politicians, rich widows, and some society figures. Al played on the elevator and often on the flat roof of the hotel, which he accessed by a metal staircase. His friends

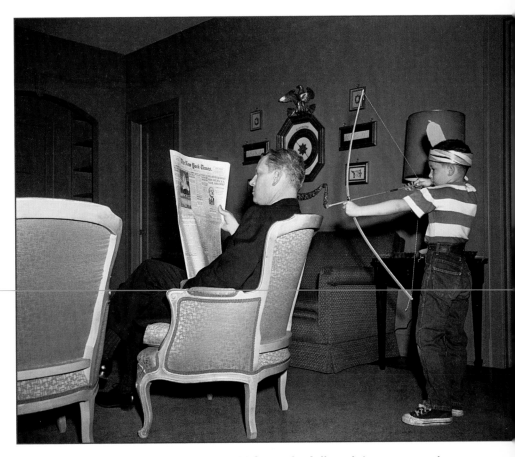

In this June 1954 image, young Al Gore playfully points an arrow at his father in their room at Washington's Fairfax Hotel.

were known to spend time up there throwing around a Frisbee until the wind took it from them. They would also drop plastic bags filled with water on passing cars and lower toys tied with strings over the hotel doors to try to bop unsuspecting guests on the head.

Pauline strived to make the hotel seem like home by baking her own bread and making breakfast. The morning was the only time that young Al and Albert Sr. got a little time together for horseplay. Pauline usually made pancakes and gave the father and son a little bonding time before school. Reports differ here about whether Al had a leisurely or rushed morning. Someone who worked in the hotel lobby reported that Al would gulp down breakfast and run at breakneck speed to the elevator and out of the hotel lobby at almost exactly the same time every day in order to catch the bus to St. Albans School. Yet in an article for the *Nashville Tennessean,* Pauline reported that breakfast was always leisurely and that her son would be taken to school by private car every morning at 7:55 A.M.

Pauline used the kitchen table at The Fairfax as a source for her son's political education. "Al always listened to what his father was doing and how his father was doing it," she told the *Nashville Tennessean.* If they had important people over for dinner, she would make a space for him at the table. "I selected guests for us; if it so happened there was a great guest who was a good conversationalist and the issue was proper for me and my son, then I would see if I could wedge Al in." Once, when two cousins were over, she asked them which of them was going to be president. Although all three of them were sitting at the table, Al's cousins realized immediately that the question was directed only at him.

While Al's Washington upbringing was an education in politics and playing with friends whose parents also created policy that affected the entire country, his other, more rural upbringing was in stark contrast. This rural upbringing, however, also seemed to be engineered by his political father and his politically minded mother.

GROWING UP IN CARTHAGE

"I grew up on a farm, I know farm life and I am a farmer," Al Gore said during a campaign speech in Tennesse, as reported by author Hank Hillin. "I'm happy that my parents gave me a good education . . . but if you're a boy and you have the choice between the eighth floor of a hotel and a big farm with horses, cows, canoes and a river, it was an easy choice for me."

Until Al was eight or nine and started to attend the prestigious St. Albans school in Washington, he grew up in Carthage, Tennessee, and attended Carthage Elementary school. Although his parents worked in Washington, there were plenty of people hand-picked to care for him. His grandparents lived next door, and the tenant farmers who worked on Gore Farms, the Thompsons, also played a role in his early upbringing.

Al loved to sleep at his grandparents' house, even when his parents were in Carthage. They had a large feather bed that lay beneath a painting of a biblical story, Daniel in the lion's den. The painting made such an impression on him, that after his grandmother died, he hung it in his office in the White House. In his grandparents' house, he learned how to read, and his grandfather even taught him to spell his first word—*green.*

Al and his buddies had much more space to play in Carthage than he and his Washington friends had. They camped out in pup tents, rode horses, canoed in the Caney Fork River, and raised cows that they would show at the county fair. His teachers at Carthage Elementary School were very much impressed with their young student. One of his teachers, Miss Smotherman, even admitted that she wasn't quite prepared for a student like him. "His intelligence was frightening," she told Hillin. "Al Gore Jr. was so mature and advanced I had to almost look at him to see whether he was a child or an adult."

He had good grades and was well-behaved. One of his teachers, John C. Davis, said that he was "a dutiful son," according to David Maraniss in his 2000 book *The Prince of Tennessee: The Rise of Al Gore.* Davis also reported that he thought "it was almost unnatural for a boy to be that well behaved." Another of his teachers reported that it seemed Al had grown up very early. When they heard the news that he was running for president in 1988, they all assumed that he would win and were all very proud of their former student.

When his parents were at work in Washington and when his grandparents were not around, Al lived with Alota and William Thompson, who lived in the tenant house on Gore Farms. They cared for him for more than 10 years during every vacation period, as well as for an entire year when he was seven. Even as an adult, Gore has said he still considers Alota his "second mother." The

Thompsons's house was quite different from The Fairfax Hotel or even the big house on Gore Farms. It had no indoor plumbing or bathrooms. Mrs. Thompson said, "That didn't make a bit of difference to young Al. He didn't care. It didn't bother him." Albert Sr. seemed to want his son to rough it.

Albert Sr. was concerned that his son would grow up never learning how to do hard work, so he asked William Thompson to keep him busy, and Mr. Thompson complied. He reported that the younger Gore worked right along with the other farmhands in the fields. Al was no troublemaker and followed orders dutifully, and Mrs. Thompson kept him supplied with his favorite things to eat: hamburgers and vegetables.

When Albert Sr. was at the farm, he made sure that Al worked either in the tobacco fields or with the cattle from sunup to sundown. Albert Sr. himself was not averse to farm work. In fact, he was quite adept at it, having been raised his entire life on the farm, and not, like his son, only during school holidays. People who worked alongside Albert Sr. said that he was incredibly strong and could rip open feed bags with his bare hands, a major feat.

Young Al always had one special summer project, dictated by his father, to complete. One summer it was to clear an entire field that had become overgrown with small trees and shrubs. As a tool, Al had been given only a small hand axe. His then-girlfriend said that the tool was insufficient for the task at hand, but he cleared the field that summer anyway—and without complaint.

When his father wasn't there, Al had more of a break. Whenever his sister Nancy was around, he and his friends, who worked alongside him on the farm, would finish their chores early so that they could accompany Nancy and her friends for some afternoon leisure time. Nancy made sure that Al and his friends were included. And as Al got older, his leisure time naturally started to include hanging out with girls.

In the summer of 1962, 14-year-old Al asked his friend's sister, Donna Armistead, who was then 16, out on a date. She was hesitant at first, wondering what her high-school friends would think about her going out with someone two years younger, but she finally agreed to date Al. Not long after their first date, he asked Donna to go steady. The two remained a couple throughout Al's high-school years despite being separated for months at a time during the school year. Donna noted that every time he returned to Carthage, it would take a few days to get the stiffness of Washington out of his body, but soon he would relax and start walking like a native Tennessean again. Albert Sr. gave Al money only when it was absolutely necessary, so the young couple didn't have much money for dates. Still, he did have a car—an old one that he drove until it practically fell apart. Though Al was book smart, he wasn't mechanically inclined. One day when the car got a flat, he couldn't get the spare out until Donna flagged down some of her friends to help him. Considering the age of the vehicle, it was probably a miracle that they never had to deal with anything worse than a flat tire while they were on the road.

Al and Donna broke up shortly before he went to Harvard. Donna reported that while he was at St. Albans, Al wrote her two

NANCY GORE AND THE PEACE CORPS

Al Gore Jr. was groomed for the presidency since his infancy, and his sister Nancy was also brought up to be involved in politics. When John F. Kennedy, still a senator, encouraged students at a Massachusetts college to become involved in volunteer work in developing nations, the idea of the Peace Corps was formed. At first, it was an informal group in which Nancy worked as a volunteer. After Kennedy was elected president, Albert Sr. took her to the Oval Office to meet with the president to be part of a discussion about the formal founding of the Peace Corps. In 1961, Kennedy signed the executive order that began the official start of the group.

letters a day and called her once a week. The other students at St. Albans didn't seem to notice much, except for one, who found Donna's reply letters to Gore. Upon hearing that the teen had read them, Al punched him in the nose. Donna never visited Al in Washington, but while he was in Tennessee, the two spent a lot of time together at each other's homes and at the Baptist Church that they both attended.

Al managed to keep his Carthage and Washington lives very separate, almost as if there were two different people living his life. The experiences never seemed to cross paths, and the people surely didn't. None of his Carthage friends ever visited him in Washington, and Alota Thompson told author Hank Hillin that all the time Al lived with her in Carthage, "he never mentioned the first person in Washington."

Al excelled academically at Carthage Elementary. Yet, at St. Albans, his grades were good, but he was never quite at the top of the class. His girlfriend in Carthage thought that he was an excellent basketball player, saying once that he probably could have gotten a basketball scholarship to any school. Yet, his athletic prowess at St. Albans appeared less stellar. He played many sports in high school, but did well only because he put in a lot of time and effort. Al was not a natural athlete, which became very apparent when he joined the basketball team in college. He sat on the bench for most of the season while the guys with far better abilities played.

During the school year, he played on hotel rooftops with the sons of politicians, and in the heat of the summer, he worked the farm with the sons of farmers. Albert Sr. thought the two worlds fit together perfectly. "I think a boy, to achieve anything he wants to achieve, which would include being president of the Unites States, oughta be able to run a hillside plow," he once said as he watched his son work the fields.

Early Influences

OBSERVING CONSERVATION

On Christmas Eve in 1968, one of the astronauts aboard the spacecraft Apollo 8 took a picture of Earth from space. The photo was called "Earth Rise" and shows Earth rising above the horizon of the Moon, the way we might see the Moon rising over Earth's horizon every night. The photo became famous. After seeing the photo, Pulitzer Prize-winning poet, and former Librarian of Congress Archibald MacLeish wrote, "To see the Earth as it truly is, small and blue and beautiful in that eternal silence where it floats, is to see ourselves as riders on the Earth together. . . ." The photo changed attitudes that people had about the planet. Over the next few years, the Clean Air Act and the Clean Water Act were passed, and the first Earth Day was celebrated.

But by 1968, young Al Gore had already made his own observations about the world that we lived in and why it needed to be properly cared for. As a boy on the farm, he walked every inch of it with his father. Albert Sr. showed him how to prevent the topsoil from eroding by using rocks and branches to stop rivulets of water from washing it away. It was an early lesson about how simple effort can prevent later problems. He noticed that people who lived off the land, as farmers did, were far more aware of all the ways that Earth needed to be cared for and often automatically took care of Earth by ensuring that rivers didn't overflow the banks, by not

The famous image of an Apollo 8 astronaut's view of Earth rising over the moon made people think differently about our planet's role in the universe.

Biologist and author Rachel Carson wrote numerous books and articles about conservation issues, including *Silent Spring* in 1962. That book about pollution in our environment, which Gore read as a teen, is widely credited with launching the environmental movement.

polluting water, and by using every resource to its fullest extent so that there would be less waste. These early lessons in conservation formed the way that the younger Gore looked at Earth and his understanding of why it was important to make those efforts that benefit the planet.

When Al was about 14 years old, his mother read a book called *Silent Spring* by Rachel Carson. His mother believed that the message of the book was that human civilization had the power to seriously harm the environment. She believed so much in Carson's message that she read the book to Al and his sister Nancy. Al said that the book made a huge impression on him and his sister. "The way we thought about nature and the Earth was never the same again," he wrote in the young people's edition of *An Inconvenient Truth*.

Silent Spring was published in 1962, despite efforts by the chemical and agricultural industries to stop it by filing various lawsuits. The book's most famous chapter, "A Fable for Tomorrow," is Carson's prediction of a day when all life in an American town is silenced by the effects of using DDT, a toxic pesticide. The book was blasted by a *Time* magazine reviewer, who called Carson's book oversimplified and said that she used many generalizations, questioning her research. Carson held her ground. In June 1963, President Kennedy formed a committee to investigate the claims in Carson's book. The findings of the committee supported Carson's conclusions and publicly vindicated her. People were forced to admit that using DDT was harmful. The chemical was eventually banned from use. Seven years later, in 1970, the U.S. Environmental Protection Agency (EPA) was created. In *An Inconvenient Truth*, Gore said, "*Silent Spring* came as a cry in the wilderness, a deeply felt, thoroughly researched, and brilliantly written argument that changed the course of history. Without this book, the environmental movement might have been long delayed or never have developed at all."

Carson's book was controversial, but it was effective in getting people to think differently about the environment and about the ways that human beings affect the cycle of life when they introduce foreign elements, like chemicals, into the environment. It certainly made Pauline Gore think about how the environment was being affected by people, and she passed that concern on to her children.

Al was still in high school at the time that Pauline shared *Silent Spring* with him and Nancy, but several years later, he was still clearly affected by the message of the book. In 1968, he decided to take a course at Harvard University in natural sciences. His professor's name was Roger Revelle.

Dr. Roger Revelle, pictured here at a Washington, D.C., joint Senate-House Atomic Energy Committee hearing in May 1957, was a teacher and trusted advisor to Al Gore.

For years before Al Gore came into his classroom, Revelle had been interested in changes in the environment. In 1957, Revelle participated in the International Geophysical Year, which ran from July 1957 to December 1958. The International Council of Scientific Unions oversaw a series of coordinated observations about geophysical phenomena around the world. Scientists observed and measured such things as wind velocity in the Antarctic, ground movement, and the movement and composition of glaciers. To participate, Revelle and a researcher named Charles David Keeling set up a research station at the top of Mauna Loa, a large volcanic mountain on the big island of Hawaii. They launched weather balloons and analyzed

ENVIRONMENTALIST RACHEL CARSON

Rachel Louise Carson was born on May 27, 1907, in Pennsylvania. Her mother, a former teacher, taught her about the birds and plants that surrounded her rural home. She took to writing early, penning a story inspired by her older brother in the military, called "A Battle in the Clouds." For her senior paper in high school she wrote about people squandering natural resources. Carson found her calling, writing about biology, when she attended the Pennsylvania College for Women. She then earned a master's degree in marine biology at The Johns Hopkins University. Carson became a marine biologist with the U.S. Fish and Wildlife Service. She wrote articles for her job and also for publication in magazines.

Rachel Carson's writing was well known for being hauntingly beautiful in description and meticulously researched. Before *Silent Spring*, she wrote *Under the Sea Wind*, *The Sea Around Us*, and *The Edge of the Sea*, all of them about how everything in nature is connected. She could easily trace the connection of sea mollusks the amount of carbon dioxide in the air. After a few years, Revelle and his research partner had recorded a startling trend that showed how quickly the amount of carbon dioxide in the atmosphere was building up. Revelle also became concerned that the high increase in carbon dioxide would adversely affect the oceans.

When Al Gore and the rest of his classmates entered Professor Revelle's Harvard classroom, they were introduced to his findings on Mauna Loa and to the conclusions he drew, which were that the increase in carbon dioxide was manmade and that this increase would negatively affect life on the planet. Revelle's students were immediately impressed and disturbed by his findings, though

to birds and to fish in the deepest and most inaccessible parts of the ocean.

Silent Spring was written and researched over the course of four years after Carson received a letter from a friend about how the pesticide DDT was killing bird populations in Massachusetts. The pesticide was already a great concern for Carson. She had approached the magazine *Reader's Digest* 14 years before in 1945, saying that she would like to do research and then write an article for them about tests that were being conducted on DDT near her Maryland home. The magazine rejected the idea. After receiving her friend's letter, Carson, now a best-selling author, once again approached magazines with her DDT article idea. Even though she was a well-known, well-established author, her idea was once again rejected.

After *Silent Spring* was published, Carson became more widely known as an environmental activist. However, she did not live to see the U.S. Environmental Protection Agency formed, which came about, in part, because of her work. Carson died on April 14, 1964, of breast cancer. She was 56 years old.

probably none more so than Al Gore himself. Even after he left Harvard, he kept in touch with Revelle. When he became a Congressman, he asked Revelle to testify in a congressional hearing on global warming.

To this day, Gore still shows the charts that Revelle started making in 1957, but they are far more complicated now than they were when he first saw them in Revelle's Harvard classroom. The information that Revelle and Keeling gleaned during their research has now been backed up with 650,000 years of data found by scientists studying ice cores drilled in Antarctica and Greenland and with the help of computer-generated climate models as well as more recent, ongoing findings. Gore feels that the data clearly indicate what he calls "an inconvenient truth" that the climate is changing, that global warming is real, and that this is a serious threat to Earth and to the lives of everyone on the planet. In *An Inconvenient Truth*, Gore wrote about his former professor, "My life has been changed by his prescient investigation, his wisdom, his dogged clarion call to pay attention to the solid scientific facts, and, perhaps most of all, by his chart."

A DUTIFUL SON

Growing up as the son of a senator had a profound effect on Gore. Not only did his parents have political aspirations for him, but at a young age, he had access to the kinds of policy-making people and events that even the most seasoned politicians didn't. For all intents and purposes, Al Gore Jr. grew up in a political arena. As a very young boy, his father proposed legislation that would eventually help to establish the highway system that crisscrosses the United States. He sat at the dinner table while his father talked with other politicians about the merits of the bill, listened as his mother added her own opinion, and then later sat in Room 412 of the Russell Senate Office building as an eight-year-old boy, listening to his father debate where the highways would go, how wide they should be, and whether the signs should be green or blue. Al watched as his father's ideas developed and gathered momentum, weathered the criticism of opponents, and became law. His experience would be a profound lesson for anyone, but as a young child, Al may have felt the possibility for simple ideas to become law all the more powerfully.

"Making the connection between those people sitting in that room, discussing and debating, voting and enacting a law on one hand, and the bulldozers pushing the earth, and the pavement laid down, and my family being able to get home faster—that connection was very powerful," an older Al Gore said decades after watching his father's highway bill push through.

Al seemed to be somewhat awed by his father, the senator. He once prided himself on talking his father into buying him a more expensive bow and arrow toy than they had originally agreed on. When he came home after the incident, he went to his mother and informed her, "Why mother, I out-talked a Senator!" The incident also warmed the hearts of his parents, who continued to tell the story to friends and family. Though there were moments like these, Al and Albert Sr.'s relationship appeared to be strained.

Al's high school girlfriend, Donna Armistead, said that the relationship between the two Gore men was somewhat stoic. "His father would want him to listen and he would want to impress Al and it was kind of a battle back and forth," she said. Al would ask his father if he had heard about a particular topic, and Albert Sr. would say, "Why yes, son, let's discuss that." Another family friend, James Fleming, reported that "they talk about issues and politics and things that ordinary people have no interest in whatsoever, so it was very difficult to be included in [their conversations]." To make his point, he added, "Every now and then they'd ask, 'so what do you think of the Federal Reserve?' I wasn't up for the Federal Reserve. It was awful!"

Al's relationship with his father showed that he had an early need to always be well informed and well-spoken in order to make an impression on his dad. This relationship would play over and over again in Al's life as he became a meticulous researcher and

ROGER REVELLE

Roger Revelle was once described by the *New York Times* as "one of the most articulate spokesmen for science" and "an early predictor of global warming." Revelle was born in Seattle on March 7, 1909, and showed academic talent very early in his life. After dabbling briefly in journalism, Revelle turned to geology as his major field of study in college. He received his bachelor's degree from Pomona College in California and then enrolled at the University of California–Berkeley for an advanced degree. He later became a research assistant at Scripps Institute of Oceanography in La Jolla, California. During that time, he collected marine samples from the Pacific Ocean—which informed his thesis—and gained his Ph.D. Revelle then served in the Navy during World War II and became head of the Navy's geophysics branch in 1946. Two years later, he returned to Scripps and served as their director from 1951 to 1964.

In 1957, Revelle, along with a scientist named Hans Seuss, showed that carbon dioxide had increased in the air due to the use of fossil fuels, such as from burning gas in a car. He became a member of the President's Science Advisory Committee Panel on Environmental Pollution in 1965 and helped the U.S. government publish the first report indicating that the use of fossil fuels was a potential worldwide problem. Revelle then chaired the National Academy of Sciences Energy and Climate Panel in 1977. They found that carbon dioxide was staying in the atmosphere and that two-thirds of the carbon dioxide was from fossil fuel and one-third from forest cutting.

In an August 1982 article that he published in *Scientific American,* Revelle addressed the issues of rising sea levels and the role of melting glaciers and ice sheets as surface waters warmed. In 1990, he received the National Medal of Science. He told a reporter, "I got it for being the grandfather of the greenhouse effect."

continually strived to impress those around him with both his knowledge and the importance of the tasks he was undertaking. Al would learn that not everyone was as appreciative of his knowledge and receptive to his ideas as his father.

In high school, Al joined the Government Club, in which he and his classmates held political debates on Thursday evenings at 7:30 in the school library. He was part of the Liberal Party. His history teacher, Francis McGrath, said that young Al Gore was not much of an orator and that back then, his speech sounded pretty much the way it does in the present day. He read his script but didn't infuse any emotion into it. David Maraniss wrote in his book *The Prince of Tennessee* that one of his classmates called him "Earnest. Careful. Slightly dull," and then went on to say he was "hardly scintillating." The club debated current political issues such as whether China should be included in the United Nations. Al said, "We've got to let China into the United Nations . . . . With their size and population we've got to deal with them." At that time, Albert Sr. was arguing the same points in the Senate.

According to Maraniss, the only place that the younger Gore could escape the responsibility that he felt from his father's expectations was in a basement art room at St. Albans where there were exotic plants, caged birds, and classical music. There, Al put his energy into art for nine years and revealed a side of himself that was far more bold and vibrant than his personality normally showcased.

The weight of expectations took an early toll on Al's personality, as he was always "careful" as his classmates suggested. Once, on a school trip, the school bus broke down and the class had to walk to the museum. As they waited for another bus to pick them up, some other boys began to play. Al went up to one of his teachers and asked in all seriousness, "Is this the time for roughhousing?" Letting loose did not come as naturally to him as it did to the other students. This kind of formality translated into what people perceived as stiffness in Al. This perception would plague Al his entire life, though he shed some of it during college.

Making His
Own Way

HARVARD DAYS

In September 1965, young Albert Gore left St. Albans High School with a National Merit Award Scholarship and began a more adult life at Harvard University in Boston. He bought a bright red Pontiac Firebird with money he got as graduation presents and some he had been saving. It was a difficult time for the country. President Kennedy had recently been assassinated and was succeeded by Lyndon Johnson. Johnson had then won the next presidential election by promising that he would not add any fuel to the Vietnam War, but immediately after getting into office, he ramped up military troops in Vietnam. The war was unpopular, and desertion among soldiers was high. Even military experts expressed that a land war could not be won in Asia. Young men in college approaching age 18 feared being sent to war because, at the time, men of that age had to register for the draft.

The country was also suffering under a racial divide with the height of the Civil Rights movement, led by Dr. Martin Luther King Jr. Civil rights had always been an important topic in the

38

Gore family. As a child, Gore's grandparents showed him the chains that held slaves for auction in a building located near their Tennessee home. Pauline ensured that Gore's group of friends included African-American kids, and in 1959, Albert Sr., vehemently opposed the so-called "Southern Manifesto," which proposed continued segregation by trying to overturn antisegregation rulings like *Brown v. Board of Education of Topeka* (1954), which said there was no legal basis to separate school children based on race. Senator Strom Thurmond publicly ambushed Albert Sr. on the Senate floor with the Southern Manifesto bill. Thurmond called in the press to witness the event, hoping that Albert Sr. would buckle under public scrutiny. Thurmond had severely miscalculated Gore's father. He handed the manifesto to Albert Sr. and asked him to sign it in full view of the press. Albert Sr. replied, "Hell no," and gave the document back to Thurmond.

Despite the country's turmoil, Gore's life at Harvard was quite smooth. His first act of business was to run for freshman class president, and that was how he made some of his first college friends.

"I met Al Gore our freshman year when he came and knocked on the door; I opened the door and there he stood. He said, 'Hi, I'm Al Gore. I'm running for freshman council,'" remembered John Tyson, an African-American student from a well-off New Jersey family, in an interview with author Hank Hillin. In their second year, Tyson and Gore asked to room together and were granted their request. Tyson told Hillin that "the most important thing I learned from Al was not to be prejudiced myself." Tyson remembered fondly that Gore would pick up his sister from the airport and give her a ride back to school on the back of his motorcycle. After their first semester at Harvard, Gore traded in the red Pontiac for a motorcycle, which became something of a signature for him during his Harvard years. Tyson remarked that Gore's picking up his sister on the motorcycle was remarkable because Tyson's sister was black, and, at that time, the racial tension in Boston was very high.

By his freshman year, Gore also had a new girlfriend. He met Mary Elizabeth Aitcheson in his final year at a dance at St. Albans.

Both she and Gore attended the dance with other dates, but by the next day, Gore had called her up and asked her out. Mary Elizabeth's nickname was "Tipper" after the words in a Spanish ballad that her mother sang to her when she was a child. Gore ended his relationship with Carthage girlfriend Donna Armistead soon after meeting Tipper. Because he was leaving for Harvard in Boston, he encouraged Tipper to find a school in Boston to attend, and the following year, after her high-school graduation, she enrolled at Boston's Garland Junior College. She graduated two years later *cum laude* (with honors), then transferred to Boston University, where she majored in child psychology and received her bachelor's degree in 1970.

During his freshman year, Gore stayed true to the vision that had been outlined for him his entire life by entering school politics. Yet by his sophomore year, he turned away from political pursuits. He and Tipper spent a lot of time together. He also began taking some of the courses, including Roger Revelle's, that would change his outlook on the world and shape his future life as a conservationist. Among the other professors who influenced him was Martin Peretz, a professor who some students called "the school's pet radical" because of his long, bushy beard and his outlandish ties. Peretz taught a seminar called "Problems of Advanced Industrial Society," which added to the impact of Carson's *Silent Spring* and the findings of professor Revelle, making Gore look closely at the impact that people, and industry in particular, had on the environment. He also took Dr. Erik Erikson's psychology class in which they examined how a group of young boys and a group of young girls built block structures in a space. Erikson's findings, that boys sought to dominate space while girls sought to build in harmony with it, caused Gore to conclude that civilization would benefit from having "a healthier respect for female ways of experiencing the world."

Turning away from campus politics wasn't easy for Gore. Because of the heightened emotions over the Vietnam War and Albert Sr.'s public opposition to military action, people kept asking

Gore to take a stand in their political efforts. Even though Gore was also opposed to the war, he never took the bait. "The war colored our entire college experience," said Gore's classmate, Michael Kapitan. He recalled watching the news every night and hearing the weekly death toll rise. During that time, there could be two to five hundred troops dying a week. Protests popped up all over Harvard's campus, reaching their height during Gore's senior year. Gore's roommate, Tyson, recalled in *Al Gore Jr.: His Life and Career,* "Al was sought after, so to speak, by a lot of the radicals to join up with them and to give them information. . . . But when things got too far, his sense— he's got good sense—when he sensed that things were getting out of proportion—out of balance—he shied away from these people." And things did get quite out of balance with the protests on campus as the war continued and people's anger turned to rage.

Gore's dorm became a center for the radical political group, Students for a Democratic Society or SDS. The group was directly involved with, or supported many of, the Harvard protests, including a small contingent of students who attacked a car that was transporting Secretary of Defense Robert McNamara on Harvard's campus. The demonstrators rocked the car and shouted antiwar slogans at him. Two years later, a marine who was absent without leave (AWOL) named Paul Olimpieri hid at the Divinity School on campus, and several students chained themselves to him to prevent him from being taken away. Their attempt to guard him was only temporary. A year later, in 1969, Gore's senior year, Harvard faculty met to discuss the future of the Reserve Officer Training Corps (ROTC) at the school. The ROTC trained students for military service so that they could sign up when they were old enough. One hundred students staged a sit-in against the ROTC's involvement in the school, and as a result, some lost their academic scholarships.

On April 8, SDS protestors took over University Hall, an administrative building, displacing professors and deans and starting a confrontation that defined their senior year. They stayed overnight, and in the morning, three busloads of police came out with clubs to get them out by force. Gore was not involved. But his reasons to not enter campus politics may have been because the larger national political arena presented a more thorny issue. His father had just scraped by with another win for his senator's seat in 1964, and it looked very likely that his next bid in 1970 was going to be even tougher, if not impossible, to win because of his stance on the war and his refusal to sign the Southern Manifesto. Keeping quiet may have been a good way for Gore to help his dad, while ensuring a smoother path for his own eventual political career.

Gore's only political involvement after his freshman year was as head of Tennessee Youth for McCarthy. He was only involved in attending the Democratic National Convention in 1968 to see if Eugene McCarthy would be nominated. It was one of the few times he went against his father. Albert Sr. supported Hubert Humphrey over McCarthy.

Gore also stopped working on the farm during his Harvard years. Rather than spending his summers in Carthage during the four summers that he was enrolled at Harvard, he found other ways to spend his time. He took a job in Brussels, Belgium. He also took a full load of college work in Mexico City and became proficient in Spanish and became good enough to translate for his father on the campaign trail. In addition, he took courses in Tennessee history at Memphis State University and also worked one summer as a copy-boy for the *New York Times*.

Dr. Richard Neustadt, one of Gore's professors, supervised Gore's senior thesis (an 84-page document) titled *The Impact of Television on the Conduct of the Presidency, 1947–1969*. While he was at Harvard, Gore started watching more and more television, convinced that it had a profound effect on culture. He believed that future presidential elections were going to depend on how candidates could project themselves over television screens to the voters watching. He thought that candidates needed to model themselves after the charisma of President Kennedy in order to win the vote. Ironically, the impact of television and people's perception of him through a screen played a pivotal role in his political career and may have resulted in his career ending permanently.

DODGING POLITICS

Gore graduated from Harvard in 1969, *cum laude,* with a degree in government. He then had to decide what he would do next with his life. In a few months, he would be eligible to go to war. He had to decide whether he should try to dodge the draft by going to another school or by moving to Canada so that the United States

POLITICS AND TECHNOLOGY

When Al Gore wrote his senior Harvard thesis, television was the pinnacle of technology that a politician had at his or her disposal for communicating with voters. Since that time, a lot of technology has changed, thanks in part to Gore's ability to spot technological trends and take advantage of them. With the popularity of the Internet, candidates began to use Web sites to reach out to supporters to gather donations for their campaigns, to inform people about their stance on issues, and to make appearances. Once a candidate was in office, sometimes his or her Web site would still be used as a communication tool. When President Clinton was in office, his dog, Buddy, and his cat, Socks, had their own Web site.

Social media was the next to be culled into a politician's arsenal for communicating with supporters, notably Facebook and Twitter, where a politician's staff and their supporters have direct contact. The best example of a political campaign using social media to date was during Barack Obama's 2008 presidential campaign. Not only were Facebook and Twitter used, but Obama often sent mass text messages to supporters as a means of communication. Although his support grew to become quite large and won him the election, Obama's campaign was seen as a grassroots effort, mainly because of the kind of personal communication that was used between supporters, volunteers, his staff, and himself.

government could not send him to war. He felt he could not justify fighting in a war that he did not believe in. But there were other matters to consider. For one thing, his antiwar father was coming up for another election the following year, and Gore knew it was unlikely he would win. A son in the military might help his father's chances. Gore also considered his own political career. Dodging the draft would not endear him to voters. He also remembered two former classmates at Harvard who had made the decision to go to war. Denmark Groover III and Carl Thorne-Thomsen both dropped out of Harvard to join the army. Thorne-Thomsen died in the war. Despite the ridicule the two received from antiwar students, Gore said of Groover, "I admire his courage and rashness. I'm not sure at all that he didn't do the right thing." Finally, Gore considered his friends in Carthage. It was a small town, and he knew that if he avoided the draft, one of his friends would have to go in his place. Gore eventually signed up for military service.

On May 19, 1970, after completing basic training, Gore married Tipper at the Washington Cathedral. He wore a borrowed military uniform for the ceremony, which was performed by Cannon Martin, Gore's former headmaster at St. Albans. The newlyweds moved to Fort Rucker in Alabama, Gore's duty station. There they lived in a trailer park that catered to the troops. Gore helped his father campaign when he could, in full military uniform, and he worked on the base newspaper. Gore played basketball with his fellow troops and painted in his spare time.

In January of the following year, Gore was shipped off to Vietnam. He worked as a combat reporter but fortunately never had to be on the front lines. The only time that Gore ever had to carry a gun was when he pulled guard duty, which wasn't especially dangerous given his location, far from most of the fighting. Despite this, Gore felt very much affected by the war and the faces of the soldiers that he saw returning from fighting. While in Vietnam, he expressed an interest in going to divinity school to make up for his involvement in the war. One of his bunkmates encouraged him to read the science fiction novel *Dune,* which Gore later said also had an impact

Al and Tipper (the former Elizabeth Aitcheson) Gore celebrate their wedding day with Gore's parents at Washington Cathedral on May 19, 1970.

on his relationship with the environment. About five months into his tour of duty, Gore applied and was accepted to the Vanderbilt School of Divinity in Nashville. He also applied for a grant to attend Vanderbilt from the Rockefeller Foundation, which was seeking people to study religion at the time. Once he was accepted, Gore applied for early release and was granted it. He returned home from Vietnam after a short seven months.

Gore was a changed man after what he had seen and experienced in Vietnam. He and Tipper left Fort Rucker and retreated to his family's farm in Carthage. He took a job at the local newspaper that had announced his birth, the *Nashville Tennessean*, even though his parents did not veil their desire for him to go to

Al Gore (*back row, second from right*) poses with fellow soldiers in Vietnam during the war in 1971.

law school and enter politics. In the fall, he started graduate work at Vanderbilt University School of Divinity in Nashville, about 60 miles (96.5 km) from the farm. But the summer before he began studying at Vanderbilt and before his job at the *Tennessean* began, Gore, Tipper, and two of their friends drove across the United States to enjoy the sights.

They camped on Lake Michigan, and drove through the Hiawatha National Forest and the Badlands in South Dakota. They camped at Yellowstone and Yosemite National Parks and visited an art museum in Disneyland before heading back to Tennessee. Along the way, Tipper, a budding photographer, took shots of everything she saw, and one of the friends who accompanied them drew everything he could. Gore was astonished by the beauty of the country.

The stirrings of his passion for the environment, which had been mostly academic so far from books and classroom experiences, became real.

In the fall, Gore took a course on ethics taught by David Ogeltree at Vanderbilt. Ogeltree taught that people have a responsibility to make moral choices. Another course Gore took was called Theology and the Natural Sciences and was taught by Eugene TeSelle. TeSelle's belief was that there was a religious basis for people taking care of the environment. TeSelle assigned books such

Al Gore works with chief photographer Bill Preston at the *Nashville Tennessean* when Gore was a young reporter there in 1974. After returning from Vietnam, Gore took the job while attending Vanderbilt's divinity school and later its law school.

as *Our Plundered Planet,* which was about environmental destruction at the hands of people.

Meanwhile in his reporting job at the *Nashville Tennessean,* Gore struggled a little with his assignments. City Editor Frank Ritter remembers yelling at Gore to hurry up with pieces to meet the deadline. Ritter said that at the beginning, his "messy copy resembled nothing so much as a hen scratching where he had penciled in numerous corrections and additions," as reported by Maraniss in his 2000 Gore biography. Ritter worked with Gore on his writing, which got a little better with time. Gore eventually found his

THE CONSERVATIONIST PRESIDENT

Theodore Roosevelt first visited the badlands, a rugged stretch of land in South Dakota and Nebraska, in September 1883 to do big game hunting. When he arrived, he was surprised that huge herds of bison had disappeared because of excessive hunting and disease. The more time he spent in the area, the more alarmed he became at the damage being done to the land and the wildlife that lived there. He saw for himself how hunters were decimating species of animals and how overgrazing had severely decreased the grasslands, which then left less food for small mammals and birds.

When Roosevelt was elected the twenty-sixth president in 1901, he used his legislative power to protect wildlife and establish public lands. He created the U.S. Forest Service and founded 51 federal bird reservations, 4 national game preserves, 150 national forests, and 5 national parks, effectively conserving and protecting 230 million acres (93 million hectares) of public land. Many of the parks that Gore and his wife and friends were able to visit over the summer of 1971 were parks protected by Theodore Roosevelt.

niche when he began to do investigative reporting. Finally, with something that he was interested in, his writing became stronger. Gore investigated developers who were taking bribes, set up stings to catch them in the act, and then revealed them on the pages of the *Tennessean*. However, when the cases went to court, often the criminals would be let off with a slap on the wrist. It irritated Gore and led him right where his parents had wanted him all along—to law school.

"I felt intensely frustrated about policies and decisions I was writing about because I felt they were often dead wrong. But as a journalist I could do nothing to change them," Gore said. So he took a leave of absence from his job and enrolled at Vanderbilt Law School. Two years later, a political opportunity came knocking. Finally, Gore could start affecting the kinds of policies that had been frustrating him as a journalist.

ENTERING THE POLITICAL ARENA

In February 1976, Gore received a phone call from one of his colleagues at the *Nashville Tennessean*. He was told that a Tennessee congressman was announcing his retirement in the next couple of days and that someone would need to fill his spot. Gore took it as his chance to finally get into politics. By the following week, Gore had dropped out of law school, permanently given up his reporting job, and cut his hair short. He was ready to campaign.

Tipper was surprised by his decision but stood by it. His parents were glad that he was finally getting into politics, which they had steered him toward his whole life. Even his sister, Nancy, was thrilled because she always enjoyed politics and had managed their father's campaigns from the moment she was old enough to handle the job. But even with the enthusiasm of his family and all his years of preparation, on the morning that he left his house and got ready to drive to the Smith County Courthouse to deliver his announcement speech on its steps, Gore felt a wave of nausea and ran back inside the house to throw up.

Al Gore celebrates his victory in the congressional race with his father, daughter Karenna, wife, and mother in 1976.

Gore campaigned hard, and by the end of the campaign, he scored a victory by 3,500 votes over his nearest competitor. He became the youngest congressman in Tennessee history, two years younger than his father was when he first won the same seat.

AN EARLY CONSERVATIONIST

On a summer day in 1980, Gore appeared at a Girls State convention in Murfreesboro and asked how many of them thought they would see a nuclear war in their future. Nearly every girl raised her hand. He then asked how many of them thought they could change that possible future. Very few of them raised their hands. Their negative reaction was the catalyst that drove Gore to write an arms control proposal that he hoped would bring both the United States and Russia to the table to reduce the number of nuclear arms in their arsenal. In 1982, Gore finally revealed his plan, and not long after, the Russian embassy called to get a copy of it, saying it was an interesting basis to start negotiations. This was the first major political undertaking that Gore took on to try to effect change on a global scale. It would not be his last.

Gore also worked on legislation to standardize testing for infant formula. In one of his committees, he found that some infant formula companies were changing the ingredients of their products to save money, but the changes to the formula meant it was no longer nutritious. He discovered that even though the Food and Drug Administration (FDA) had received recommendations from the American Medical Association about the correct way to make nutritious infant formula, the FDA had not forced the manufacturers to adhere to any standards, nor did they ever test the products. Gore made sure that that products would be rigorously tested and that the FDA would get full access to results so that companies would be held accountable for what they produced.

In another investigation, Gore showed that he was thoughtful about how he placed blame. When he investigated the presence of a chemical agent known as "Tris" that was being put into children's pajamas to make them nonflammable, he found out that the chemical was dangerous; yet the clothing manufacturers were not informed of that fact. Gore was instrumental in passing legislation that banned the chemical and that also compensated the unaware manufacturers for their losses.

Gore was also a sponsor of the Comprehensive Environmental Response, Compensation, and Liability Act. The legislation created a "superfund" or a trust fund for the U.S. Environmental Protection Agency to clean up areas that contained toxic waste. The main question was who was supposed to pay for the cleanup efforts? Some argued that the cost should be split 50/50 with the companies who caused the waste problems and with the government. At the time that the waste was produced, no law existed to prevent the companies from creating the problem in the first place. Therefore, they did not feel that they were entirely liable. However, Gore felt that "industry not only created the risks but also enjoyed the profits derived from the sale of products whose prices did not reflect their true costs." He thought the companies alone should pay to clean up their own mess, whether it was against the law when they made the mess or not.

Even critics have noted that Gore's ability to understand technical detail and engage national attention is savvy politics. However, Gore was fighting for the same things that he had seen all along as the problems of a larger society—the kinds of things that he had read about in Carson's *Silent Spring,* that he had learned in Professor Roger Revelle's class, that he felt was his moral obligation to do something about, that he had learned at the hands of his divinity school professors, and that he saw for himself when he, Tipper, and their friends drove across the United States, camping and enjoying nature.

In 1984, Gore got another call from his colleague at the *Tennessean;* this time he was informed that a Tennessee senator's seat was soon going to become available. It was time for Al Gore to run for a new office, one in which he could influence even more change. In 1984, Gore ran for and won his first Senate seat in Tennessee. Unfortunately, his beloved older sister Nancy did not live to see him become a senator.

Road to the White House

THE INFLUENCE OF AN OLDER SISTER

Nancy Gore was quite different from her younger brother, whom she called Bo from the time he was a little boy. For one thing, she was 10 years older, old enough to dote on him when he was a young boy, going so far as to help make his meals and substitute for Albert Sr. and Pauline by attending his sporting and school events when they weren't able to do so. When they were on the farm together, Nancy always made sure that Gore didn't spend the entire day working through his father's list of chores.

The siblings were a study in contrasts. "Dark-haired and stunningly beautiful from an early age, she played family rebel to Al's conformist. . . . Nancy Gore never met a curfew she liked. According to her mother, Nancy would figure out what her parents wanted in order to circumvent their will while Al would do so in order to obey it," wrote author Bob Zelnick in his 1999 biography, *Gore: A Political Life*. While Gore was stiff, Nancy was relaxed. Where he was serious, she liked to play pranks. Gore was self-conscious; Nancy, irreverent. While their parents had different expectations for

The Gores pose for a photograph taken for their hometown newspaper, *The Tennessean,* in 1952. Nancy, 14, and Al, 4, are shown with their parents leaving their Nashville apartment.

the siblings, brother and sister simply had quite different attitudes. Gore's girlfriend Donna Armistead once told a story about having to flag down her own friends when the car that she and Gore were in got a flat in Carthage. A similar story about Nancy Gore in a broken-down car paints a sharp contrast. Nancy's car had a broken fan belt, but instead of flagging down help, Nancy removed her Christian Dior designer belt, used it as a temporary fan belt and went on her way. Her brother couldn't even get a spare tire out of the trunk.

That was another thing about Nancy. She cared very much about fashion, but her brother became noted for always wearing the same navy suit. Unlike her younger brother, "she wasn't big on rules," her friend Jim Gilliland told author David Maraniss for his book *The Prince of Tennessee.* "She wasn't big on doing things other people's way. . . . She had more fun than anybody else did." But perhaps the most defining contrast between the siblings, and one that would cause them both pain, was that Nancy was a smoker, and Gore was not.

Nancy began smoking at age 13, which was probably not surprising since the family owned their own tobacco farm. However, her parents were not pleased and tried everything they could to get her to stop, including taking away her allowance and driving privileges. Yet she would light up as soon as they were out of sight. Some friends report that Nancy was never without cigarettes and smoked up to a pack of cigarettes a day. After Nancy married Frank Hunger and they moved to Mississippi, far away from the rest of the family, her smoking was easier to hide. It took a fast toll on her though. In 1982, Nancy was diagnosed with lung cancer.

Gore was just starting his first Senate campaign. In spite of her illness and chemotherapy, Nancy still helped Bo through it. If she was well enough, she would put on a wig and make appearances with him along the campaign trail, but she would never see her brother to the election. Nancy Hunger died of cancer in 1984, just before her brother successfully won his senatorial bid.

Following Nancy's death, the family sold the tobacco farms, recognizing tobacco's health dangers, but the relationship that the

Gores had with tobacco was hard to shake. "Throughout most of my life, I raised tobacco. I want you to know that with my own hands I put in the plant beds and transferred it! I've hoed it! I've chopped it! I've shredded it, spiked it, put it in the barn and stripped it and sold it!" Gore told North Carolina voters during his first presidential campaign in 1988. And for years after Nancy's death, Gore and his family still benefitted from the proceeds of the family's tobacco farms. In 1990, for another Senate campaign, Gore accepted money from the political action committees of tobacco companies like Philip Morris and Brown & Williamson Tobacco Corporation. Conversely, when he became vice president, he and President Bill Clinton brought legislation that increased taxation on tobacco and reduced the amount of tobacco and cigarettes produced and sold in the United States. They also established smoke-free federal work-places to protect workers.

TOBACCO AND KIDS

As vice president of the United States, Al Gore recognized that tobacco companies were courting young people in their cigarette ads. He accused them of recruiting young people to replace their older cigarette-smoking clients. In the late 1990s, he and President Bill Clinton introduced legislation that would increase the price of a pack of cigarettes and force cigarette manufacturers to change their advertising campaigns so that they did not target children. For this, they had bipartisan support from politicians like Republican John McCain. They recognized that ads like Camel's Joe Camel specifically targeted children. They also conducted surveys that showed that increasing the price of a pack of cigarettes reduced the likelihood that children would smoke them.

After Nancy's death, Gore worked tirelessly to inform people about the dangers of cigarette smoking. Despite understanding the health risks of smoking the plant and lobbying against cigarette manufacturers, he always advocated for tobacco farmers, whom he identified with from years of working in the hot fields beside them. Many felt that this was an odd contrast and confronted Gore about his strange stance in blasting the cigarette while advocating for the people who produced its main ingredient, but for Gore, the product and the plant remained separate entities.

PRESIDENTIAL MATERIAL

Once in the Senate, Gore had more exposure and more influence on the kinds of environmental and civic issues that he had been bothered by all his life. More and more he began to tackle important environmental issues. In 1983, the U.S. Environmental Protection Agency (EPA) issued a report that stated that global warming was beginning to be a trend. Scientists were beginning to measure a rise in the average world temperature by several degrees over 100 years. That did not sound like very much warming, and it seemed like a long time, but according to the EPA, the impact on life on the planet could be catastrophic. Would the planet be habitable in 100 years?

After only two years in the Senate, another opportunity came knocking. Over Christmas, 1986, Albert Sr. pulled Gore aside and suggested it was time for him to run for the presidency. Albert Sr. had never considered the top job for himself. He did try for the vice president's job twice, never quite making the pick. In his father's eulogy, Gore joked about his father's goal to be the number two guy in the White House. He thought it was an interesting aspiration for a politician, saying, "Now that's humility." However, Albert Sr. saw in his son the opportunity to get into the White House that he didn't have. After a few weeks, the discussion became a family affair as Pauline, Tipper, and Gore's four children were included in the conversation. Albert Sr. felt that he would win support from members of the Democratic Party. He firmly believed that his son could win and compared him to John F. Kennedy, who was the youngest man to be president, replacing the oldest president in the nation's history, Dwight Eisenhower, in the 1960 election. Both of Gore's parents felt it was a good move, but Tipper was against it.

In the last couple of years, Tipper had come under fire for her protests against racy rock and roll lyrics. She launched a campaign against the music industry, saying that music with explicit lyrics should be clearly marked so that parents could make decisions about what their children were allowed to listen to. She and a group of other mothers established the Parents' Music Resource Center (PMRC) as a nonprofit organization to get music companies to rate the songs on their albums depending on the level of violence and offensive lyrics used. Tipper came under fire by musicians, record companies, and magazines such as *Rolling Stone* for her actions, but in the end, the PMRC was able to get record companies to put a label on albums that contained objectionable content.

After feelings had cooled, Tipper wrote a book titled *Raising PG Kids in an X-Rated Society*. The book began to sell well, and Tipper had appeared on the *Oprah Winfrey Show, Good Morning America,* and other shows as part of her book tour. "I was upset that he would even consider [running for president] at the time. His timing was atrocious. He was starting well after the other candidates and I was already away from home a great deal," she said to author Hank Hillin. Tipper worried about how the children would fare with both of their parents so busy. In the end, she decided to drop the promotion of her book.

In 1987, at age 39, Gore announced that he was considering running for president of the United States. He made the statement in the Senate Caucus Room to the press and, taking some advice from his father, he stated, "In the aftermath of eight years under President Reagan, the oldest president in our history—Americans may well decide as they did in 1960 that it is time for our country to turn to youth, vigor, intellectual capacity, and a determination to face the problems of the future with vigor and energy."

While on a campaign tour, Al Gore shakes hands with a worker leaving the New Hampshire Knitted Fabrics Factory in Manchester. The visit was planned to gain support for his run for the Democratic nomination for president on August 11, 1987.

Despite the daunting task of a presidential run, added to the fact that he was late entering the race, Gore was still committed to the work he had begun in trying to prevent nuclear war and looking at worldwide environmental changes. Between strategy meetings and calls to campaign donors and political leaders, Gore flew to the Soviet Union to speak to the group International Physicians for the Prevention of Nuclear War. The organization, made up of 150,000 doctors from all over the world, was well respected and had won the 1985 Nobel Peace Prize. In his speech to about 2,000 physicians, he said that an arms-control agreement would make it impossible for either side to increase their nuclear arsenals. That would reduce the fear of an attack and promote peace. He agreed that fear on both sides had caused both the United States and Russia to create more and more nuclear arms. In his speech, he told the physicians, "We must be doctors to each other's fears, and seek to dispel them by removing any rational basis for them."

His campaign went on, and while Gore got a lot of support in southern states, a poor showing in New York forced him to close down his campaign. He didn't take it as a loss, however, but as an indication of how far he could go considering his late start and limited funds. After the campaign ended and George H.W. Bush won the presidency, Gore was happy to return to a more quiet life with his family, but tragedy was on the horizon.

On April 3, 1989, Gore and Tipper took their son, Albert III, to the opening game of the Baltimore Orioles. Newly elected president, George H.W. Bush, was also in attendance. After the game, the energetic five-year-old got away from his parents and ran into oncoming traffic. A car knocked him 30 feet (9 meters) away, and then he slid about 20 more feet (6 m) before coming to a stop on the pavement. The Gores rushed to his side and started praying. Two off-duty nurses administered cardiopulmonary resuscitation (CPR) until an ambulance arrived. For three weeks, the Gores practically lived at The Johns Hopkins Hospital while Albert III was in grave danger. Even after their son was allowed to leave the hospital, he needed another year before he could use his right arm.

Gore said his son's accident made him really think about what he wanted to do with his life. In *An Inconvenient Truth,* he wrote, "I asked myself how did I really want to spend my time on Earth? What really matters?" During Albert III's recuperation, Gore began to write *Earth in the Balance: Ecology and the Human Spirit.* Although he had focused on many different issues in his life thus far, he now felt he needed to focus on the environment. "I realized this was the crisis that loomed largest and should occupy the bulk of my efforts and ingenuity." He began to assemble information to put into a slide-show presentation about global warming and its meaning for life on the planet. The slide show would eventually become the movie *An Inconvenient Truth* and the accompanying book by the same name.

TIPPER GORE

Tipper and Gore met in high school, and it has frequently been noted that she always supported him in every way. When he chose Harvard for college, she chose a college in Boston as well. When Gore joined the staff of the *Nashville Tennessean,* Tipper used her photography skills and secured a job there as well. However, Tipper has always had her own causes that she felt strongly about. In the 1980s, she devoted herself to getting advisory labels placed on music that had violent content or strong language. After her husband entered the White House, she was known for helping people who were mentally ill, especially the ones who were homeless and lived in the streets of Washington, D.C. Often, Tipper would go out and talk to these people, most of whom had no idea who she was, and found them the help they needed by taking them to shelters or mental health facilities. In 2002, some people encouraged Tipper to run for Congress, but she was not interested in being a politician.

THE HARDEST WORKING
VICE PRESIDENT

In 1988, Gore travelled to Antarctica to review the conclusions
of scientists who were gauging the effects of the 1970 Clean Air
Act. Following that trip, he went to Brazilian rain forests to see
the devastation that was happening there at the hands of deforest-
ers who were cutting down trees for development. For instance,
the Kayapó, an indigenous people living in the Amazon of Brazil,
saw their lives threatened by the actions of developers. Gore also
visited central Asia and the Arctic to see for himself the effects of
global warming. In 1992, he chaired the American delegation to
the Earth Summit, which met in Rio de Janiero, to set limits to
new emissions of greenhouse gases and to take other steps to allay
environmental issues. President George H.W. Bush and his administration did not agree with the findings of those at the summit,
and Gore criticized him in a speech. "The Bush administration," he
said, "[was] the single largest obstacle to progress." Gore also com-
plained that legislators and voters did not seem to be interested in
the facts that he was uncovering about climate change and the way
those changes would impact life on the planet. Along with other
politicians, he tried to pass legislation that would limit carbon
dioxide emissions in the United States, but the legislation failed.

In 1992, *Earth in the Balance* was published. In it, Gore said,
"we need to think strategically about our new relationship to the
environment." By now, the link between climate change and human
action had been well documented, and Gore wanted people to
think carefully about their effect on the environment. He said that
by curbing population growth and finding technological solutions,
we could significantly reduce the damage we were already causing.
He understood that education and worldwide cooperation were
going to be the key in solving the problem. Unfortunately, Gore did
not anticipate that educating the public about the environment was
going to bring the kind of negative attention that it did. Although
many saw the implications of what he described in his book, very
many others did not agree and did so both publicly and loudly.

Gore's political detractors used his environmental stance as a target, saying that his research and evidence were flawed, and often they called him a hypocrite. In his 1999 book, *Gore: A Political Life,* author Bob Zelnick said, "Gore had yelled 'Wolf!' when there may well have been nothing worse than a tame old dog in the field." The voices of Gore's detractors would become a constant thorn in his paw.

To make matters worse, Robert Revelle, Gore's former Harvard professor and the man who had first shown him the data on increased carbon dioxide in the atmosphere, died in 1991, leaving behind some unanswered questions about his research. Before his death, his name appeared in an article in the magazine *Cosmos* titled *What to Do about Greenhouse Warming: Look Before You Leap.* In it, Revelle with two other authors wrote that despite increased carbon dioxide in the environment, science could not conclude that it was affecting the climate. The article also said that drastic action to reduce emissions could cause global poverty. The article seemed to negate the things that Revelle had taught Gore so many years before at Harvard. There was some question as to whether Revelle had actually been a coauthor or had only signed on in his last days without really participating in the writing of the article. No one will ever know his true feelings about it because his death came too soon after the article was published for those questions to be addressed.

Also in 1992, George H.W. Bush was running for reelection. Gore did not enter the presidential race again, but a young governor from Arkansas, Bill Clinton, did. He won the Democratic nomination and turned to Al Gore to be his second in command.

"I personally selected Al Gore from a large number of other qualified democrats to be the vice-presidential candidate on our ticket," Clinton wrote in the introduction to Hank Hillin's *Al Gore Jr.: His Life and Career.* "Al was the first person I asked, and I'm happy and proud that he accepted." Clinton called Gore "a modern day patriot." When the two families, Clinton and his wife Hillary and Gore and Tipper, first set out on the campaign trail together, they hit it off immediately. Clinton later said that he felt that between

Vice-President-elect Al Gore applauds as President-elect Bill Clinton holds up a "Fat Lady Sang" sweatshirt celebrating their win at the Old State House in Little Rock, Arkansas on November 4, 1992.

Gore and his wife, he had two vice presidents. It was a relationship that sometimes became thorny between Gore and Mrs. Clinton, but eventually the two settled into separate roles in the Clinton White House because they were interested in different issues.

The Clinton/Gore ticket won the election in 1992, and the two men embarked on a team leadership effort that was unlike any president/vice-president relationship that the White House had ever seen. For one thing, Gore was given far more control over issues than any other vice president in history. He and Clinton had weekly meetings during which they would discuss their joint approach on issues and legislation. Clinton went so far as to tell everyone that when Gore spoke, he was speaking for the president as well.

The primary goal of the Clinton administration was to work toward a safe environment, to increase the technological capabilities of the United States, and to ensure the country's ability to compete with the rest of the world. Clinton felt that Gore had both the intellect and the vision to help him accomplish those goals. Throughout the campaign, Gore talked about the importance of the information superhighway. To him, it was the computerized equivalent of the interstate highway system that his father had helped to create in the 1950s. One of the first initiatives undertaken by the Clinton administration was an 18-page document called *Technology: The Engine of Economic Growth*. The administration hoped to jump-start the economy again by focusing less on military matters and more on civilian issues, starting with an emphasis on new technology. The Clinton administration was willing to redirect up to $76 billion in federal research funds to "spur industrial innovation," according to a November 1992 *New York Times* article. The shift toward technological research and development was also right up Gore's alley.

A New Millennium

THE POLITICAL PARTNER

Time and again, Gore and Clinton worked together to resolve issues and push initiatives in the Clinton administration. Gore advised Clinton on all the environmental and technological issues and was able to get the president to back them, though not always as aggressively as he might have liked. One of the first initiatives the two took on was to push research in technology.

On Earth Day 1993, President Clinton announced that the United States would sign the Framework Convention on Climate Change that the Bush administration had refused to sign after the summit in Rio de Janeiro. In 1993, Gore also got Clinton to propose a BTU tax. BTUs, or British thermal units, are a measure of the amount of energy being used. The BTU tax would encourage people to be more aware of how much energy they were using and hopefully to cut down their consumption of energy. The House passed the bill for creating this new tax, but the Senate did not. Gore was so sure that the facts behind his BTU tax plan would get people to see the light that he didn't do the necessary groundwork

66

to gather support and momentum for the bill. Environmentalists were disappointed with Gore's attempt, and this incident would not be the only time that he failed to please fellow environmentalists.

Gore had long stated his ire over the Bush administration's refusal to participate with the goals and findings of the Earth Summit. The administration said that there was not enough evidence of global warming to recommend that they reduce carbon emissions in the United States. Now that Gore was in the White House, environmentalists expected that he would work with President Clinton to reduce emissions. Unfortunately, the Clinton plan called for voluntary action only by businesses. That meant businesses were not required by law to reduce emissions, so it was likely that not many of them, if any at all, would make the necessary changes. Environmentalists were further surprised when the Clinton administration did not require American car makers to build cars that used less fuel.

Two years after Clinton and Gore won the White House, Republicans took control of the House of Representatives during midterm elections. One of the goals of House Republicans was to curb environmental laws that were already in place. Gore advised the president to take a stand against their anti-environment actions. Environmental groups supported the White House, and no laws were changed.

Clinton and Gore faced the Republicans again during the 1996 election against Bob Dole and Robert Kemp. The Clinton/Gore ticket won an easy victory and didn't miss a step with their continued policy work. The following year, Gore attended an important environmental conference in Kyoto, Japan. The purpose of the conference was to create binding treaties with industrialized nations, requiring them to set and maintain standards for reducing carbon emissions. Some argued that it was unfair that nations such as China, India, Pakistan, and Brazil were exempt from the binding treaties, but representatives of those countries argued that industrialized nations like the United States had one or two people in every car while their people were riding buses. If they were to reduce their emissions further, they said, there wouldn't even be a bus for them to take.

With Glacier National Park as his backdrop, Vice President Al Gore stresses the dangers of global warming on September 2, 1997. "Global Warming is no longer a theory," Gore told the audience. "It is a reality. And it is time to act."

In the end, the disagreements, though fierce, managed to smooth out. Environmental activists felt that there was a narrow victory won but that the Kyoto Protocol, as it was called, did not go far enough to protect the environment. An article in the *New York Times* reported that businesses were going to have to change the way that they produced and used energy as environmental issues "should be taken into consideration in planning and investing for the long term." Since that time, businesses have begun to make significant changes in the way they use energy and in the way that they produce and market products to consumers. Many of them have found that the changes that are good for the environment also reduce costs for the companies and give them a good public image.

Gore helped to draft the Kyoto Protocol. With this proposed international environmental treaty, countries then needed to agree to ratify the treaty themselves. It meant that they had to agree to reduce the emissions of six different kinds of greenhouse gases in their countries, including carbon dioxide. In his remarks, Gore said, "Our fundamental challenge now is to find out whether and how we can change the behaviors that are causing the problem." On his return to the United States, Gore tried unsuccessfully to persuade the United States to ratify the treaty. Once again, his facts were met with doubt. Although 141 countries have ratified the treaty since the meeting in Kyoto, the United States remains the only advanced nation that has not. The U.S. Senate unanimously voted against ratification because they said the treaty asks only industrialized nations to reduce their carbon dioxide emissions.

Although Kyoto was a good step in the right direction, some scientists worry that the requirements of the Kyoto Protocol aren't enough to make a difference to the environment. In his 2006 book *The Weather Makers,* Tim Flannery says, "If we are to stabilize our climate, Kyoto's target needs to be strengthened twelve times over." More recently, Gore recognized that Flannery was correct. As early as 2007, Gore himself felt that the United States needed to reduce their carbon dioxide emissions by 90 percent by 2050.

The other issue brought up in Kyoto was raised by the United Nation's Intergovernmental Panel on Climate Change, which found that global warming would cause extreme weather conditions. And as early as 1991, Senate majority leader George Mitchell warned that "climate extremes would trigger meteorological chaos—raging hurricanes such as we have never seen, capable of killing millions of people; uncommonly long, record-breaking heat waves; and profound drought that could drive Africa and the entire Indian subcontinent over the edge into mass starvation." As predicted, there have been extreme weather conditions in the last decade, such as more violent hurricanes like Hurricane Katrina in 2005 and drought in African nations beginning in 1999 and continuing throughout the early part of the century, affecting 16 million people, according to United Nations Children's Fund (UNICEF) reports.

Working toward reducing the effects of climate change was not the only thing that Gore did as vice president. In 2000, he paved the way for a series of initiatives to protect and preserve a number of different habitats while still being considerate of the people who lived nearby, such as farmers. He directed agencies to establish a network

A BOY AND HIS WINDMILL

Al Gore long advocated for alternate forms of energy, such as wind energy. The objections to making the change have come from many who think it's too hard to accomplish, and those who believe the costs of building windmills and solar panels will be astronomically high. However, one young man in Malawi, Africa has shown that getting wind energy is a matter of simple determination and finding the right scrap parts.

William Kamkwamba and his family live in Malawi, a country in Africa. At the beginning of the century, the African continent was rocked with a massive drought, which killed thousands of people. Although William and his family survived, it was not without great loss. His father had lost most of his crop, and William had been forced to drop out of school because his family could no longer pay the tuition. Rather than being idle, William went to the local library to find books to read. The library was little more than a room with a couple of shelves filled with any books the librarian could find, but it was enough for William. A friend who still attended school tried to keep him up with schoolwork by showing him what he learned every day. One day, William came across a book about windmills. It was written in English, not his native language, so he wasn't able to read it, but by looking at the pictures he was inspired to build one for himself. He thought that the windmill could power a water pump and allow his father to plant two crops a year. This would prevent them of ocean conservation areas, authorized plans to protect Hawaii's coral reefs, and directed the U.S. Environmental Protection Agency to take further steps to arrest the pollution of beaches, oceans, and coasts. In addition to protecting oceans, he secured the money necessary to acquire untouched desert land in southern California in

William Kamkwamba is photographed at the African Leadership Academy, while attending school in 2009, in Johannesburg, South Africa. At the age of 14, the former school dropout designed and built a windmill to power his family's home in Malawi.

from going hungry again. With determination and scrap parts that he hunted all over his village to find, William finally completed his windmill. Though ridiculed as "crazy" by his neighbors, the windmill worked. William brought free electricity to his house through wind power. People charged their cell phones from his windmill, and William became famous for his ingenuity and determination.

order to preserve it. He also announced a partnership with the state of Ohio to help farmers protect their lands and improve water quality. He worked with several heavy-duty U.S. engine manufacturers to come up with more fuel-efficient trucks in order to improve fuel economy, cut greenhouse gases, and reduce air pollution.

By the end of their second term, the Clinton/Gore team had affected everything from promoting conservation in farms, to reducing childhood lead poisoning, to building communities that promote a better quality of life along with economic growth. As President Clinton's second term was coming to a close, many people were looking to Gore as the natural successor to the presidency, but not everyone thought he was the best candidate for the job.

A SECOND PRESIDENTIAL BID

Gore did not announce that he would run for the office of president right away. He waited until 1999, just a year before the elections to make his announcement. By then, he had a few rivals waiting in the wings. Bill Bradley, a former Democratic senator from New Jersey, was his main rival in the Democratic primaries. Yet once Gore won the nod from fellow Democrats, another candidate took some of the wind from his sails. Green Party candidate Ralph Nader ran as an Independent and challenged both Gore and his Republican rival, George W. Bush, son of former president George H.W. Bush. Nader and Gore actually agreed on many of the same issues, particularly those concerning the environment. But Nader and his supporters did not feel that Gore had done enough in his time in the White House to make a lasting and effective change. Gore supporters wanted Nader out of the race, fearing that he might take away support from Gore that he needed to win the election against Bush. And in the end, it was a very close contest.

Because the race was tight, every detail came into play in deciding who the winner would be. Ironically, one of the things that did Gore a disservice was his commitment to technology.

In the Clinton White House, Gore was able to follow up on his continued commitment to advancing technology that he first documented an interest in when he wrote his senior thesis at Harvard. In May 1989, while still in the Senate, Gore introduced a bill to connect government, universities, and businesses to a small group of computer networks. This would become the early Internet. The bill that he sponsored while he was a member of the Commerce, Science, and Transportation Committee would ensure that this burgeoning technology had enough financial backing for it to grow. The bill passed in 1991. *Wired* magazine saw Gore's longtime support of technology as a boon. They called Gore "a genuine nerd with a geek reputation running back to his days as a futurist 'Atari Democrat' in the House [of Representatives]." Atari was one of the first video game systems created. In general, the feeling of those intimately involved in the creation of new technology saw the vice president as an important asset to their work. As time wore on, though, there were those who chose to ridicule Gore's work in promoting technology. In his second term as vice president, he took a direct hit that he was never able to shake off.

In a 1999 CNN interview with reporter Wolf Blitzer, Gore said, "During my service in the United States Congress, I took the initiative in creating the Internet." The media had a field day with that statement. Reporters blasted Gore for taking credit for the term "creating the Internet," saying that he was asserting that he had laid the technological groundwork for it, when, in fact, he was talking about laying down the *political* groundwork for it, as shown in his inclusion of ". . . during my service in the United States Congress." A 1999 report titled *He Invented the Internet (Sort of)* in *Wired News,* an online subsidiary of *Wired* magazine, made an article about the statement, and it was then picked up by nearly 5,000 articles in the weeks that followed. Those in the technology world didn't bite the bait that reporters were throwing out. They understood what Gore meant. The two people who actually helped to build the infrastructure for the Internet, Robert Kahn and Vinton Cerf, came to Gore's defense in an October 2000 article for *The Register,* saying, "Al Gore was the first political leader to recognize the importance of the Internet and to promote and support its development. No one person or even small group of persons exclusively 'invented'

Al Gore shakes hands with then–Republican presidential candidate George W. Bush before a televised debate on October 3, 2000.

the Internet. . . . But as the two people who designed the basic architecture and the core protocols that make the Internet work, we would like to acknowledge VP Gore's contributions." They added, "No other elected official, to our knowledge, has made a greater contribution over a longer period of time."

Although many people publicly defended Gore, including Newt Gingrich (then Speaker of the House and a long-time Republican), Gore was cast in a negative light when the Republican brass used *Wired News'* misquoted line "invented the internet" to put words in his mouth and to basically paint him as an exaggerator and a liar. In a close political election, this was the kind of negative distraction that could cause disaster. Even a decade later, people still erroneously believed that Gore said he invented the Internet.

Adding to this, in the debates between Gore and Bush, Bush appeared more relaxed, whereas Gore appeared stiff. It was the same kind of stiffness that his teachers and classmates had noticed in him during their debates at St. Albans. On camera, even Gore's makeup looked overdone, and it colored the way that people perceived him. It was ironic that his senior thesis at Harvard was on precisely how a presidential candidate's performance before a television audience could make or break the candidate's political career. It seemed to be coming true for Gore, though not in the way he would have liked. While George W. Bush appeared personable, relaxed, and even jovial, Gore's stiffness, formality, and seriousness on camera made some voters uncomfortable with him as a candidate. Still, on Election Day, Gore had a good chance to be victorious over his opponent, and he thought it would soon be over. Yet what happened next, no one could have predicted.

THE LONGEST ELECTION NIGHT EVER

On November 2, 2000, when people went out to cast their votes, they could not have imagined that the election would drag out into a gut-wrenching fight to the finish. At the end of the night, nobody knew who had won the election. The state of Florida had technical problems with the ballots. People who had intended to vote for Al Gore had instead voted for another candidate, so many votes were not properly counted in some counties. A legal battle began the very next day between the Democrats who wanted to have a recount and the Republicans who wanted the votes to stand as they were. The reason for the legal intervention was that Gore had won the popular vote, but Bush had won Florida's electoral votes, making him the overall winner. If the recounted votes in Florida favored Gore, he would have won the Florida electoral votes and the presidency. The Florida Supreme Court allowed the recount

WHAT HAPPENED TO THE ELECTRIC CAR?

A car that runs on electricity rather than fossil-burning gas would be considered a huge step in the right direction by environmentalists like Al Gore. In the 1990s, there was such a car in production, but it soon disappeared, much to the disappointment of many who wanted to buy it. So, why did the electric car disappear in the first place?

In 1990, the California Air Resources Board saw a General Motors car prototype called the EV1. It was a fully electric car, which meant that it didn't use gas and that it didn't have any harmful emissions. In response, the California Air Resources Board created the zero emissions vehicle mandate, which required that 2 percent of all cars sold in California be emission-free by 1998 and 10 percent by 2003. In 1996, General Motors launched the EV1 for sale to consumers. The EV1 was extremely easy to care for. It did not need gas or oil changes. It also didn't need to have mufflers, and it rarely needed brake maintenance. The main care for the vehicle was refilling the washer fluid and rotating the tires.

to go forward, but lawyers for the Republican Party kept challenging the decision. The legal war kept the outcome of the election from being determined for five weeks. Finally, Gore conceded to Bush on December 13, 2000, after the U.S. Supreme Court got involved and stopped the recount. Once again, Gore would not be president.

"This certainly wasn't an easy time," Gore wrote in *An Inconvenient Truth,* "but it did offer me the chance to make a fresh start—to step back and think about where I should direct my energies." Just as he did after his son's accident, Gore took some time to really

Not only was maintenance extremely easy, but it was extremely cheap. By 1998, however, the cars began to disappear from the market. Automakers said they stopped making the cars because no one wanted to buy them. Yet all of the cars they made had been bought, and there was a long waiting list of customers. Fortunately, someone chose to investigate, wondering why consumers wouldn't want a car that was cheaper to run and maintain than a regular gas-powered car.

In 2006, director Chris Paine released his documentary *Who Killed the Electric Car?* based on his investigations about why the cars were pulled from production. He found out that because the cars did not need replacement parts as often or products such as motor oil, filters, spark plugs, and brakes, auto makers and parts manufacturers were going to lose money. Pressure from the billion-dollar oil industry, which produces gas for traditional cars, sealed the deal. No EV1s were produced after 1998. The electric car was essentially dead. Paine's documentary won several film festival and writing awards in 2006 and 2007. It is listed on Netflix's Top Ten list of "important movies you should see."

Al and Tipper Gore, along with his running mate Connecticut senator Joe Lieberman and his wife Hadasah, are greeted by well-wishers as they leave the Old Executive Office Building in Washington, D.C., after Gore conceded the race on December 13, 2000.

reflect upon what he wanted to do next. Once again, he knew he wanted to focus on the environment. It was a cause that he was going to dedicate all his waking hours to, but first, Gore would take a much-needed hiatus from public life.

LIFE AFTER THE WHITE HOUSE RUN

For the first time since he entered the House of Representatives as a junior congressman, Gore retreated from public life completely. Rumors abounded about how he was spending his time, but when he emerged, he seemed to be a more focused man. He announced that he wanted to teach. Therefore, he began a series of lectures about journalism at universities around the country. He specifically wanted to talk about how journalism intersected with technology. His first lecture was at Fisk University, a historically black college in his native Tennessee. He also lectured at Columbia University in New York, the University of California in Los Angeles, and Middle Tennessee State University. His lecture at Columbia University was titled *Covering National Affairs in an Information Age*. Gore felt that the role of journalists to report responsibly and to let the facts speak for themselves had eroded in the information age as news reports came faster and faster without all of the necessary fact-checking, a process which took time. Reporters were putting out news quickly at the expense of substance, Gore felt, and he wanted to address that with students. At the same time, Gore revealed that he and Tipper were working on a book about American families and the challenges they faced in a modern world. This book was published in 2002 as *Joined at the Heart*.

Most politicians who find themselves voted out of office usually find work as the board member of a corporation, and Gore was no exception. He turned solidly to his interest in technology that began when he was a student at Harvard and signed on as a consultant

POPULAR VOTE VS. THE ELECTORAL COLLEGE

When Al Gore Jr. lost the 2000 election even though more people had voted for him, he wasn't the first person in U.S. history to have been in that position. In 1888, Benjamin Harrison became president despite losing the popular vote to Grover Cleveland by 100,000 votes. The reason this happens is because of electoral votes. Each state has a certain number of electoral votes based on their population. There are 538 electoral votes in all. A candidate needs to win 270 electoral votes to win the presidency.

for the Internet search engine Google and became a member of the board of Apple, Inc. Still plagued by news reports that painted him as sour and stiff, Gore became further disenchanted with the way the media portrayed events. Therefore, he began to develop his own television network called *Current TV*. The goal of Current TV was to give back power to the people by allowing anyone to create content via podcasts and to upload them to Current TV's station. They could then be viewed and put into regular rotation based on voter reviews. Although Gore created Current TV, he rarely appeared on his own network. He preferred instead to use MoveOn.org as his vehicle for communication. Rather than appearing in front of people as he had in the past, his writings about current events and political policies were broadcast via MoveOn and sent to the inboxes of millions of people. Gore was beginning to manipulate the media to spread his message, rather than allowing the media to manipulate him as they seemed to have done throughout the 2000 election.

As Gore became more of a private citizen and George W. Bush settled into his presidency, Gore became one of the loudest and most listened to Bush detractors, mainly because the voters who had supported him during the 2000 election felt an affinity to the guy who had lost in such a public and crushing way, and many of them felt that Bush had unfairly taken the White House.

Postelection Gore appeared far more relaxed and jovial than he had ever been throughout his years in politics, and many wondered where this affable Gore had been during the most important election of his life. As he continued to comment on the policies of the Bush administration, speak out about journalism and technology, and show his slideshow about global warming, Gore was quickly winning popularity among people, not as a politician, but as someone who had something important to say about the environment and world events. In an ironic twist of fate, the private Gore was beginning to have more impact on the discussion about ecology, media, and politics than the politician Gore ever had.

A Private Servant

SERVING THE PEOPLE AGAIN

At a dinner party in 1989, Gore first showed his slideshow about global warming. At the time, he had only a series of slides, based on the ones by Professor Revelle, to go on and the data that he had gathered from scientists. Gore continued to show his slides to fellow senators and the media, sometimes stunning them with information about the rapid warming trend Earth was experiencing and sometimes not. After his election loss in 2000, Gore decided to return to his slideshow, but this time he wanted to take his message to the general public.

Gore had, over the course of his political career, enjoyed disseminating information through Town Hall meetings, where he got to have face-to-face time with the people he represented and with the voters whom he encouraged to go to the polls. Although he worked in Washington, D.C., for many years, he regularly returned to Tennessee on weekends to meet with people and listen to their concerns. He now felt that it was time to take his own concerns about the planet to those same people that he had met at Town Hall meetings, as well

Standing in front of a screen displaying northern hemisphere temperatures, Al Gore delivers an address attacking the Bush administration's environmental policies on January 15, 2004 in New York's Beacon Theater.

as to many others. In a few months after the election, Gore took his slideshow on the road across the United States and then to the world.

By 2001, Gore's slideshow had become more sophisticated. Rather than just a series of slides of data and pictures, Gore had an interactive show that he could display on large screens. When he began showing the data, the final graph—one that showed the steep climb in temperature over the last couple of decades—had to be flipped up so that viewers could see the incredibly sharp rise in temperature. It had a dramatic effect on people who had never seen the data before. Using his new computerized slides and large-screen format, Gore chose an even more dramatic method of showing Earth's climb in temperature. As he showed the graph and eventually got to modern times, he would climb into a cherry picker, and then the graph would move sharply upward as Gore's cherry picker took him up several feet to the top of the screen so that everyone could see how far and fast temperatures were rising.

Because Gore had gained so much popularity from being the popular vice president who lost, he had a lot of visibility. Everyone wanted to know what the former vice president was going to do next. Many people who had voted for him felt sympathetic to his postelection fate and tried to support him by encouraging him to run again in 2004. Their slogans that read "Gore in '04!" went unheeded as Gore concentrated on his message. He knew that he had the ear of the people and that what he told them was astonishing.

Gore's message—that everyone had to act immediately to avert a global catastrophe—was backed by scientific data and unbelievable pictures of dwindling glaciers, polar bears trapped on floating pieces of thinning ice, and dying coral reefs. He said that even though disaster might not happen in our generation, disaster was imminent if people continued to live their lives exactly as they had been without concern for their impact on the planet. Global warming would severely affect our children and grandchildren. Slowly, people were beginning to hear his message and heed it, but Gore still wanted to reach more people.

"It was Tipper who first suggested that I put together a new kind of book with pictures and graphics to make the whole message easier to follow, combining many elements from my slide show with all of the new original material I have compiled over the last few years," Gore said in *An Inconvenient Truth.* In May 2006, Gore's slideshow became the book *An Inconvenient Truth,* which was released in conjunction with a documentary of the same name. Gore's slideshow now had a world release in movies, eventually on DVD, and in bookstores and libraries. His message was out for all to see.

MAKING *AN INCONVENIENT TRUTH*

It wasn't Al Gore's idea to turn his slideshow into a movie. In 2004, film producers Laurie David and Lawrence Bender attended the premiere of the film *The Day After Tomorrow*, a movie starring actor Jake Gyllenhaal. It was about a young man trapped in New York following a sudden and catastrophic climate change. Gyllenhaal's father in the movie, played by actor Dennis Quaid, is a climate scientist, who tries to warn the government that climate change will become a serious problem if they don't act quickly. The impossible follows as a series of storms change global weather overnight, plunging the planet into another ice age. After the premiere, David and Bender saw Gore's slide show and thought he should make it into a documentary. They contacted director Davis Guggenheim about the project, and though he was skeptical at first, he changed his mind after seeing Gore's slideshow for himself. More than two years later, Guggenheim, along with the former vice president, accepted the Oscar for best documentary. The book that Tipper had encouraged her husband to write based on the information in his slide show became a companion piece for the film.

GETTING RECOGNITION

The *New York Times* compared *An Inconvenient Truth* with Gore's 1992 book *Earth in the Balance,* saying that it was easier to read and that Gore's love of charts had been put to better use in this book than it had in his previous one. They also felt that Gore allowed the images in the book to speak more powerfully than he ever could about snow loss on peaks like Africa's Mount Kilimanjaro. Additionally, "Mr. Gore does a cogent job of explaining how global warming can disrupt delicate ecological balances, resulting in the spread of pests, increases in the range of disease vectors, and the extinction of a growing number of species." Because the book was so easy to read and the movie painted him as a more relaxed figure, the two vehicles were making him into a celebrity. More than ever, he appeared on the news and on television programs where he promoted the book and the movie and presented his conservation message. Gore appeared more relaxed, accessible, and sympathetic than he had throughout the campaign or during his entire political career, and he became a more likable and easy-to-listen-to public figure. Reporting for the *New York Times,* Michiko Kakutani felt that Gore's book "might even push awareness of global warming to a real tipping point—and beyond." Kakutani may have been right. The number of companies and individuals who are trying to reduce their carbon footprint or their adverse effect on the environment has increased tremendously in the last decade.

Early in 2007, just a few months after *An Inconvenient Truth* was released in theaters, Gore and his director, Davis Guggenheim, won the Oscar for Best Documentary Features for 2006. In his acceptance speech, Gore said, "We need to solve the climate crisis. It's not a political issue, it's a moral issue." Melissa Etheridge's song, "I Need to Wake Up," from the Gore documentary, won Best Song. "I have to thank Al Gore for inspiring all of us," Etheridge said in her acceptance speech. In a February 2007 *Washington Post* article, Guggenheim said, "Everywhere I go with [Gore] they treat him like a rock star." Gore's former campaign manager, Donna Brazile, told the Web site Politico.com that "Gore's political stock is hot right

Producer Laurie Davis, director Davis Guggenheim, and producer Lawrence Bender (*left to right*) join Al Gore in accepting the Best Documentary Feature award for *An Inconvenient Truth* at the Kodak Theater in Los Angeles on February 25, 2007.

now." Despite further cries for Gore to run again in 2008, Gore avoided the subject.

The rest of 2007 and into 2008 were going to be very busy for the former vice president. In the fall of 2007, Gore won the prestigious Nobel Peace Prize along with the scientists of the Intergovernmental Panel on Climate Change. Some reporters wondered in their columns what global warming had to do with world peace, but Gore understood that rising temperatures would eventually cause drought in some parts of the world. As rivers dried up, food and water would become scarce. In other parts of the world, a rise in temperature would cause Arctic and Antarctic ice to melt, raising the sea levels, which would force people who live on coasts to flee their homes. People who are seeking refuge due to shortages in food and water or flooded land would put a great strain on the rest of the world's land and resources, causing

Actor Leonardo DiCaprio stands with Al Gore on stage at one of the Live Earth concerts held at Giants Stadium in New Jersey on July 7, 2007.

violence and conflict. The Nobel committee felt that doing something about climate change before it is too late was one way of promoting peace.

In 2007, Gore also partnered with Emmy-winning producer Kevin Wall to start the foundation Live Earth. Their first project was to create a series of concerts called *Live Earth: The Concerts*

CARSON AND GORE

In 2002, the anniversary edition of *Silent Spring* was released, and Gore was asked to write the introduction. In it, he noted how Carson's detractors had attacked her personally, using the fact that she was a female scientist against her by saying that her writing was "hysterical." Gore also noted that prior to the book, the word *environment* was not a word familiar to politicians or to anyone in charge of public policy. Gore remarked on Carson's courage in addressing the problem in the first place despite being warned against writing about it and on her further courage in facing those who challenged her after the book's publication. Gore understood that Carson's words profoundly affected people and changed their thinking forever. However, public policy has still not met the challenges that Carson outlined in her book.

Gore might well have been writing about himself. With his first book *Earth in the Balance,* Gore introduced himself as a public policymaker very much concerned with the impact that people have on the environment. The barbs came soon after and continued to increase as Gore became more outspoken on environmental issues. Even though public policy still has not risen to Gore's standards, he continues to work for a greener planet, all the while enduring those who seek to tear him down, just as some critics tried to do with Rachel Carson.

for a Climate in Crisis. The concert was held on July 7, 2007, on 7 continents and was broadcast in 132 countries to 2 billion people. The goal was to create a global community dedicated to solving the problems of global warming. After the very successful concerts, the work of Live Earth continues to sponsor events that engage the community to act favorably toward the environment.

After Gore's Nobel Peace Prize win, even more people rallied behind Gore for a 2008 presidential run. There was even a Web site, DraftGore.org. This time, Gore coyly avoided discussing his intentions in public, making some believe that he might be considering entering the political scene once again. Yet Gore was still incredibly busy with his own agenda, teaching people about the climate crisis. As a matter of fact, it might have been a genius move on Gore's part not to come right out and make his intentions known. The sense of mystery kept people's eyes on his every move, and in early 2008, his every move had everything to do with the environment. In March, he testified at global warming hearings in both houses of Congress. Then in May, his new book *The Assault on Reason* hit bookstores.

Gore further banked on his rock-star status and began to make television appearances on popular shows such as *The Daily Show* and *Futurama* to talk about climate change. It was a way to reach more people in a relaxed way. He was also parodied in television shows like *South Park,* further evidence of the kind of popularity he had gained. Now, when people think about a spokesperson for climate change, they think about Al Gore. He has become a popular icon, as recognizable as any other public figure, from politician to pop singer. But that kind of fame also came with a price.

ATTACKING THE MESSENGER

While there were many who were hearing Gore's message and heeding his advice to be more cautious about their impact on the globe, there were many others who didn't believe in his message and who went so far as to ridicule him for it. Because this was a long-term cause for Gore, the ridicule started early. During the Clinton/Gore 1998 campaign against George H.W. Bush, then President Bush called Gore "Ozone Man" and said that if Clinton and Gore won the election, the population would be out of work and "up to our necks in owls." During the Clinton administration, there was widespread prosperity in the United States. Gore never forgot the average person in his quest for finding methods of combating climate change. He advocated for "green" industries so that people could find jobs in areas such as wind farming and solar panel and electric car manufacturing.

Immediately after Gore's Academy Award win, Drew Johnson of the Tennessee Center for Policy Research released a statement saying, "As the spokesman of choice for the global warming movement, Al Gore has to be willing to walk the walk, not just talk the talk, when it comes to home energy use." In his statement, he alleged that Gore's house used 20 times more electricity than the average U.S. home. Johnson failed to note that Gore's house is also the site of his offices and his wife's offices and that some of their electricity is due to Secret Service and extra security precautions that need to be taken for a former vice president of the United States. Johnson also failed to note that the house was very old and less energy efficient than newer homes or that Gore had purchased blocks of "green energy," meaning that rather than using energy from carbon-emitting coal like most homes, they used energy that came from wind power and methane gas, both renewable sources. Gore had also undertaken a vast renovation to the more than 100-year-old Nashville house, installing solar panels on the roof and making other renovations to make energy consumption more efficient. At the time of Johnson's statement, renovations were not complete, so all of the added benefits were not yet in effect.

Confronted with the facts that he left out of his statement, Johnson replied, "The energy he receives into his house is no different than what I receive into my house." He added to *Washington*

Post reporters, "He doesn't have a green power line hooked to his house."

The problems didn't end there. The government in the United Kingdom planned to show Gore's documentary in every school, but a judge halted the plan, saying that Gore's film had gross exaggerations. Justice Michael Burton said that Gore's "apocalyptic vision" was biased, based on his political beliefs, rather than resulting from scientific fact. Although Burton presented no scientific facts of his own, he said, "The fact that it received an Oscar this year for best documentary film, a powerful, dramatically presented and highly professionally produced film" was evidence that it wasn't scientific but rather "built around the charismatic presence of the ex-vice president." The United Kingdom's online newspaper *Times Online* said that the justice agreed in general with Gore's statements but felt that his conclusions were too extreme.

Gore even came under scrutiny for his earnings. Nick Allen, reporting for the United Kingdom's newspaper the *Telegraph,* said that Gore was profiting from climate change because he invests in technology companies that are working to make the electricity grid more efficient. Allen argued that because the U.S. Energy Department was spending billions in grants, some of which would go to utilities that use "green energy" like the company that Gore invested in, he stood to profit from the policies that he was helping to create. The media began calling him a "carbon billionaire."

In a hearing on clean energy legislation in 2009, Republican congresswoman Marsha Blackburn remarked to Gore: "The legislation that we are discussing here today, is that something that you are going to personally benefit from?" Gore replied, "I believe that the transition to a green economy is good for our economy and good for all of us, and I have invested in it."

The fact is that Gore began investing in green energy long before people believed that anyone could make a profit from it, back when he was still a laughingstock for even bringing up the issue and politicians were giving him mean nicknames. Gore added that "every penny" of his profit from his green energy investments has gone to the nonprofit Alliance for Climate Protection, which works to find solutions to climate change problems. In a subsequent television interview on ABC, Gore said, "I am proud to have put my money where my mouth is for the past 30 years." He also added that "though that is not the majority of my business activities, I absolutely believe in investing in accordance with my beliefs and my values."

In Gore's most recent book, *Our Choice,* he specifically addressed media disinformation that he felt was confusing the issue of climate change. He specifically targeted television personalities Glenn Beck, Lou Dobbs, Sean Hannity, and Rush Limbaugh. He wrote that most scientists agreed that global warming was real and was created by human activity by the late 1980s, but the oil and coal companies, who made their money on burning fossil fuels that greatly increase greenhouse gases, didn't want that information to become popular knowledge. Beginning in 1989, oil companies began funding groups that they set up to run a misinformation campaign. These groups had names like the American Council on Science and Health and the Global Climate Coalition. The groups put out ads that said things such as "Who told you the earth was warming . . . Chicken Little?" and "Some say the earth is warming. Some also said the earth was flat." As more and more people began to believe the effects of climate change, the tactics of the groups changed. Now rather than saying climate change wasn't happening, they said that it was happening but that it wouldn't have any serious effects.

There are still Web sites like globalwarming.org that claim that climate change is not real. The intention of Web sites like these is to lure people into believing that the organizations behind these Web sites are treating the issue fairly. However, their articles don't contain all of the facts. They report that only "some scientists" agree that global warming is real, when in reality, the vast majority of scientists agree that global warming is not only real, but a major threat to human lives. Some of these sites advertise anti-Gore books like *Not Evil, Just Wrong* and project what they believe will be the enormous cost of changing our energy sources. Many Web sites like these include information from scientists who say there is no evidence of global warming. Naomi Oreskes and Erik Conway's 2010 book, *Merchants of Doubt,* discusses the scientists who don't believe in global warming. The authors found that some of the scientists who believe there is no global warming also believed that there was no hole in the ozone layer and that tobacco did not cause cancer. Despite the evidence that the depletion of the ozone layer was, in fact, a major problem, some scientists called it a myth or stated that it was a fixable problem. Fortunately, politicians created laws that helped the situation, and people and businesses changed the kinds of products they used. These actions have helped to repair the ozone layer. In 1953, a study showed that cigarettes caused cancer. Once again, there were scientists who said that was also a myth. Now, the link between cigarette smoking and cancer is an undisputed fact. However, until 1993, the tobacco industry was still trying to weaken scientific claims that tobacco was bad for people's health.

Gore said that the worst thing to happen in the arena of misinformation was President George W. Bush's appointment of Philip A. Cooney as the person in charge of environmental policy in 2001. "Before that, Cooney had worked as a lobbyist at the American Petroleum Institute, where he had been working for years to deny global warming," Gore wrote in his book *An Inconvenient Truth.* "Now it was his job to write government policy. Of course, he used that position to write policy that favored the oil industry." Gore went on to say that during the eight years of the Bush administration, scientific reports were changed and censored to reflect more positively on the oil and coal industries. "Our own government has been misleading us," Gore stated.

Continued Effort

BUILDING ANOTHER INFRASTRUCTURE

More than half a century after his father set in motion the project to create the country's interstate highway system, Al Gore, who helped lay the legislative groundwork to establish the Internet, is laying the groundwork for a new plan. He says we now need to create an energy super grid that uses renewable forms of energy such as solar and wind power and that we need to reduce our dependency on coal and foreign-bought oil. Gore underscores that using fossil fuels like oil and coal is increasing global warming and that it is depleting the U.S. economy. In 2008, standing before a packed audience at George Washington University's Constitution Hall, Gore addressed both the economics and the environmental challenges of the problem. "We're borrowing money from China to buy oil from the Persian Gulf to burn it in ways that destroy the planet," he said. "Every bit of that has to change."

Gore believes that the change in our energy use needs to happen within the 2010s. Both China and Australia are already actively working toward those goals. The United States, if it doesn't act now,

Al Gore shares ideas with then-president-elect Barack Obama in Chicago on December 9, 2008.

will be left in the dust. Former President Bill Clinton and Gore spoke in 2009 at an energy summit at Washington's Newseum. According to Clinton, moving to the smart grid is not just a good idea for the planet, it would also be good for the economy. "We have to maximize the impact of this economic recovery plan," Clinton said. "I hate to be like a Johnny one note, but the sexiest things to talk about are what we're going to do with clean energy." Speaker of the House Nancy Pelosi agreed, saying, "The grid issue is central to all that we do. The world is crying out for America to take the lead. People are doing their part, but we must lead the way."

President Barack Obama is in favor of changing the way that we use technology not only to better the energy infrastructure of the country but also to wean ourselves off foreign energy sources and the use of coal, which is destructive and polluting. Gore and Clinton praised Obama's economic recovery package, saying that it would allow the country to better deal with climate change by using renewable energy such as wind and solar.

The goal of the smart grid is to get the energy from the places where wind energy and solar power production is the greatest—in the middle of the country—to the east and west coasts where the largest cities that require the most energy are located. "We have to be sure we do it in a way that helps us use the grid in the smartest possible way," Senate Energy Committee Chairman Jeff Bingaman told the Web site Politico.com. Those in favor of moving forward are not as aggressive as Gore, who believes that the goal should be to cut our dependency on oil and the loans to buy oil within 10 years. They believe that moving forward should be more cautious. Philip R. Sharp, president of Resources for the Future, said, "It's extremely important to have people like Al Gore who are pushing and pressing the edge of the envelope," he told the *Washington Post* after a Gore speech in July 2008. "But at this point I don't think there's anyone in the industry who thinks that goal, as a practical matter, could be met. This is not yet a plan for action; this is a superstretch goal." Gore does understand, though, that moving forward for the better requires getting others on board, and that it may need a little caution. In his book *Our Choice,* Gore talked about the super grid and quoted an African proverb: "If you want to go quickly, go alone. If you want to go far, go together."

THE WORK AHEAD

In a 24-year political career, and for several years since leaving the political arena, Al Gore has worked to change the way that people use the planet. He has successfully changed the thinking of many people who are now more careful about how they use energy, and he is working with politicians and in a private capacity to change public policy so that people can live in a more environmentally sound world without sacrificing their quality of living. But doing so has been a long, hard slog, and his work continues.

In 2000, when he was still vice president, Gore proposed government help for communities to build rail systems that would reduce dependence on gasoline. His "Keep America Moving Initiative" pledged $25 billion to build high-speed rail systems and to convert city and school buses to cleaner-burning fuel. In 2010, one of the first systems to start building with the federal funds was Florida.

THOMAS EDISON

The inventor of the light bulb may not seem like an environmentalist. After all, Edison's incandescent light is the least efficient and the most costly to use. However, Edison believed in renewable energy. He tried to create wind turbines to generate electricity, and he worked with his friend Henry Ford, inventor of the assembly line and car manufacturer, to develop a car that would run on rechargeable batteries. Edison knew that the supply of coal and oil would eventually run out and that people would be looking for new sources of energy.

Thomas Edison stands beside his original dynamo, a device for creating a steady supply of direct current (DC) electricity, in his New Jersey lab around 1906.

In 1931, just before he died, Edison said to his friends Henry Ford and Harvey Firestone, who was a tire manufacturer, "I'd put my money on the sun and solar energy. What a source of power! I hope we don't have to wait until oil and coal run out before we tackle that."

Gore was there to help them break ground on the construction of a high-speed train that would run from Orlando to Tampa at speeds above 120 miles (193 km) per hour. A second phase of the project would connect Miami. Florida expects that the first trains will be running by 2014.

Gore supports the creation of new jobs from the use of more clean energy. In a June 25, 2009 blog entry, he cites a *New York Times* article that states, "Two more reports from a broad coalition of environmental groups and research institutes suggest that clean-energy investments have the potential to kick-start the economy and employ millions of workers—particularly those at the lower end of the economic scale." The article goes on to say that an investment in clean energy could create an increase of "1.7 million American jobs and significantly lower the national unemployment rate." Following the economic crisis that began in 2008, everyone was watching carefully the rise in the unemployment rate, and many were concerned that Gore's plan to revamp the energy grid would be entirely too costly in a fragile financial environment. However, the research seems to be proving him right. "It's no secret our economic crisis and the climate crisis are linked, and so are their solutions," wrote Gore in the same blog post. "We now know that the legislation to repower America will cost less than $175 per family. The time for action is now."

Gore's follow-up to *An Inconvenient Truth* was the book *Our Choice*, which won him a Grammy Award in 2009 for best spoken-word album. In the new book, he outlines an easy-to-follow plan for helping to solve the climate crisis. In *An Inconvenient Truth*, the information he presented was overwhelming to some, and many felt hopeless, wondering how such a huge crisis could be averted, so he addressed that in *Our Choice*. He wrote, "Today most Americans not only understand that global warming is real but want to do something about it. That's what this book is about."

Gore lists the sources of global warming pollution in his book as coal mining, industrial waste, melting permafrost (a permanently

Al Gore promotes his book *Our Choice* at a Barnes & Noble
bookstore in New York City on November 4, 2009.

frozen layer of earth), coal-processing plants, crop and forest
burning, land transportation such as trucks and cars, oil production, landfills, fertilization with chemicals similar to the ones that
Rachel Carson warned about in *Silent Spring,* and agriculture.
He advocates for using carbon-free energy like geothermal plants,
solar and wind energy, water, and nuclear power plants. Gore uses
maps to show the plentiful sources of these kinds of energy that
exist in the United States. If we tap into them, we won't have to
use the land-destroying methods of coal mining and oil drilling,
and we won't have to put more pollution into the atmosphere by
burning these fossil fuels for energy. All is not bleak, according
to Gore.

"In 2009, after years of delay, the United States finally began to lead the world in fighting global warming," he wrote in *Our Choice*. He noted that the United States had increased organic farming, changed the way that we traveled and the buildings we lived in, and planted trees to replace some of the ones lost to deforestation. In 2009, the United States, along with other nations of the world, assembled in Copenhagen, Denmark, at a climate conference to talk about how all nations could work together to solve the problems of global warming. Gore wrote in his book: "2009 was the turning point. It was the start of some of the biggest changes the world has ever seen." But that's what it was, a start. Gore is still continuing to work to help solve the climate crisis, and he is still speaking to people to educate them about the problems the planet faces and to encourage change.

Gore's legacy in working on the climate crisis may have grown much larger than he anticipated. Nearly 3,000 people have now been trained in giving his global warming slideshow, so that many more people can be educated about what is happening. In addition, the Web site climatecrisis.net has recorded the direct impact of Gore's message on how people run their businesses and live their lives. The site says that more than 106,000 tons (96,161 metric tons) of carbon were offset the year after the documentary *An Inconvenient Truth* was released. That is the equivalent of 225 million miles (362 million km). In addition, more than 4,200 tons (3,810 metric tons) of carbon were offset when people switched to energy-saving light bulbs. The U.S. government has also undergone changes: The House of Representatives appointed a committee on Energy Independence and Global Warming, and President Obama created a new position, Assistant to the President for Climate and Energy.

Still, the work that Gore has accomplished to inform people about climate change may have come at great personal cost. In June 2010, just two weeks after their fortieth wedding anniversary, he and Tipper decided to end their marriage. The decision was mutual, and according to news reports, they had begun to have very separate lives with him away from home so much.

Despite the personal setbacks, Gore continues to work to educate people about environmental issues. He is also working to create laws that would benefit the planet and to help people understand what they need to do to help. As he said in his book *An Inconvenient Truth,* "It is our only home. And we must take care of it."

How to Get Involved

The following organizations can provide more information on global warming and climate change.

U.S. Environmental Protection Agency
http://www.epa.gov
"The mission of the EPA [U.S. Environmental Protection Agency] is to protect human health and to safeguard the natural environment." This organization studies problems using laboratories throughout the United States, develops and enforces regulations involving the environment, and informs Americans about their role in helping to protect the environment.

Live Earth
http://liveearth.org/en/liveearth
Built on the belief that "entertainment has the power to transcend social and cultural barriers to move the world community to action," the people associated with Live Earth organize several events driven to educate people and get them involved in environmental issues.

National Resources Defense Council
http://www.nrdc.org
Founded in 1970, the National Resources Defense Council calls itself the most effective environmental action group in the country. Its purpose is to protect Earth and all its inhabitants, including the natural systems on which life depends.

Stop Global Warming
http://www.stopglobalwarming.org
This is a nonpartisan group dedicated to making changes in the environment as individuals and as a global community. On their site, they publish a list of simple "action items" that anyone can do to reduce their contribution to global warming.

Chronology

1948	Albert Arnold Gore Jr. is born on March 31 in Washington, D.C.
1965	Gore meets Elizabeth (Tipper) Aitcheson. He enrolls at Harvard University where he meets Roger Revelle, one of the first scientists to measure carbon dioxide in the atmosphere.
1969	Gore graduates with honors from Harvard on June 12. He enlists in the army in August, during the Vietnam War.
1970	Gore marries Tipper on May 19 at the Washington National Cathedral.
1971	Gore is honorably discharged from the army and enrolls at Vanderbilt Divinity School. He takes a job as a reporter at the *Nashville Tennessean*.
1973	Gores' first child, Karenna, is born on August 6.
1974	Gore takes a leave of absence from the paper and enrolls at Vanderbilt University Law School.
1976	Gore wins his first election to Congress.
1977	The Gores' second child, Kristin, is born on June 5.
1979	The Gores' third daughter, Sarah, is born on January 7.
1982	Gore outlines a nuclear arms control plan to the House of Representatives in March. On October 19, Albert III is born.
1984	Gore's sister Nancy dies in July. In November, Gore runs for his first Senate seat and wins.
1987	He launches his first presidential campaign.
1988	On April 21, Gore withdraws from the presidential race.

1989	After a baseball game on April 3, Albert Gore III is struck by a car and seriously injured. In May, Gore introduces a bill to expand development of the Internet.
1992	Gore's first book, *Earth in the Balance,* is published in January. Gore attends the Earth Summit. Bill Clinton chooses him as his running mate in the presidential election. The Clinton/Gore team wins.
1993	Gore is sworn in as vice president of the United States.
1994	On Earth Day, Gore launches the globe program that uses the Internet to teach students about the environment.
1996	Clinton and Gore are re-elected for a second term.
1997	Gore helps to write the Kyoto protocol but fails to get the support of the U.S. Senate.
1998	Albert Gore Sr. dies on December 5.
2000	Gore runs for president and wins the popular vote but loses the electoral vote. George W. Bush becomes president.
2001	Gore teaches politics and media at several universities.
2002	Gore edits and adapts a slideshow with climate change data and begins to tour with this new multi-media presentation. He and Tipper have two books published, *The Spirit of Family* and *Joined at the Heart.*
2006	The documentary *An Inconvenient Truth,* based on Gore's multimedia presentation, is released in May. The book *An Inconvenient Truth* is released simultaneously. Gore founds the Alliance for Climate Protection and The Climate Project.

2007   The Young Reader's edition of *An Inconvenient Truth* is published. In February, Gore wins the Academy Award for *An Inconvenient Truth.* In May, Gore publishes another book, *The Assault on Reason.* In June, he backs a campaign to switch off London's lights for one night in a mass carbon-saving event. In July, Gore helps to organize Live Earth, an all-day, seven-continent series of concerts to increase global awareness of climate change. On October 12, he is presented with the Nobel Peace Prize as a cowinner with the Intergovernmental Panel on Climate Change for their work concerning global warming. In December, Gore speaks at the United Nation's climate conference in Bali.

2008   A special-interest group launches an advertising campaign claiming that Gore's Tennessee home uses 20 times more electricity than that of the average U.S. home. Gore becomes chairperson of the TV channel *Current TV.* Along with the Alliance for Climate Protection, Gore launches a $300 million campaign to help Americans force politicians to make policy to reduce emissions. In May, an Italian opera house announces their work on an opera based on *An Inconvenient Truth.*

2009   Gore testifies to the Senate foreign relations committee about global warming. His book *Our Choice* is published.

2010   In an email to friends, Gore and Tipper announce the decision to end their marriage, two weeks after their fortieth anniversary.

Glossary

campaign Competition between political candidates for a public office

conservation Carefully using natural resources such as land and water to prevent waste and to reduce usage

dignitaries Persons who hold a position of honor

embassy The official home and offices of an ambassador who represents his or her country

environment The combination of climate, soil, and living things that make up a home or community

geophysical Dealing with the branch of earth science that pertains to physical processes and phenomena about Earth and atmosphere

legislation Rules and laws

negotiations The act of working with another person or party to settle a matter

nomination The process of naming a person to be a candidate for election to political office

pesticide An agent used to destroy pests

phenomena An event or fact that can be observed

ratify To approve or confirm something

solar Anything that comes from or is related to the sun

toxins Poisonous substances that come from living creatures

treaty An agreement or an arrangement that is made after a negotiation

Bibliography

"A Heated Exchange: Al Gore Confronts His Critics." *The Wall Street Journal.* March 5, 2009. Available online. URL: http://blogs.wsj.com/environmentalcapital/2009/03/05/a-heated-exchange-al-gore-confronts-his-critics/

Agre, Phil. "Who Invented 'Invented'?" *Red Rock Eater Digest.* October 17, 2000. Available online. URL: http://web.archive.org/web/20040603092645/commons.somewhere.com/rre/2000/RRE.Al.Gore.and.the.Inte1.html

Aldred, Jessica and Lauren Goodchild. "Timeline: Al Gore." *The Guardian UK.* Available online. URL: http://www.guardian.co.uk/environment/2007/oct/12/climatechange1

Allen, Nick. "Al Gore 'profiting' from climate change agenda." *The Telegraph.* November 3, 2009. Available online. URL: http://www.telegraph.co.uk/earth/environment/climatechange/6496196/Al-Gore-profiting-from-climate-change-agenda.html

Boehlert, Eric. "*Wired* Owes Al Gore an Apology." *The Huffington Post.* April 28, 2006. Available online. URL: http://www.huffingtonpost.com/eric-boehlert/wired-owes-al-gore-an-apo_b_19980.html

Broad, William J. "Clinton to Promote High Technology, With Gore in Charge." *The New York Times.* November 10, 1992. Available online. URL: http://www.nytimes.com/1992/11/10/science/clinton-to-promote-high-technology-with-gore-in-charge.html?sec=&spon=&pagewanted=print

Cillizza, Chris and Matthew Mosk. "War on Warming Begins at (Al Gore's) Home." *The Washington Post.* March 1, 2007. Available online. URL: http://www.washingtonpost.com/wp-dyn/content/article/2007/02/28/AR2007022801823.html

Fehrenbacher, Katie. "Al Gore: The Smart Grid Is Key." *Earth2tech.* November 19, 2009. Available online. URL: http://earth2tech.com/2009/11/19/al-gore-the-smart-grid-is-key/

Flannery, Tim. *The Weather Makers: How Man is Changing the Climate and What It Means For Life on Earth*. New York: Grove Press, 2001.

Forbes, Sarah. "High Speed Rail Projects Start in Florida." *The Sustainability Ninja*. January 29, 2010. Available online. URL: http://www.sustainabilityninja.com/sustainable-transportation/high-speed-rail-projects-start-in-florida-99811/

"Gore: Universities have important role in sustainability." *Harvard Gazette*. Available online. URL: http://news.harvard.edu/gazette/story/2008/10/gore-universities-have-important-role-in-sustainability/

Gore, Al. *An Inconvenient Truth: The Planetary Emergency of Global Warming and What We Can Do About It*. Emmaus, PA: Rodale, 2006.

————. *Our Choice: How We Can Solve the Climate Crisis, Young Readers' Edition*. New York: Melcher Media, 2009.

Harris, Bonnie. "Gore offers $25 Billion for energy efficient transit." *LA Times*. June 30, 2000.

Hillin, Hank. *Al Gore Jr. His Life and Career*. New York: Birch Lane Press, 1988.

Hillstrom, Laurie Collier. *Al Gore*. Detroit: Gale Cengage Learning, 2009.

Kahn, Robert and Vinton Cerf. "Al Gore and the Internet." *The Register*. October 2, 2000. Available online. URL: http://www.theregister.co.uk/2000/10/02/net_builders_kahn_cerf_recognise/

Kamkwamba, William and Bryan Mealer. *The Boy Who Harnessed the Wind: Creating Currents of Electricity and Hope*. New York: HarperCollins, 2009.

Landau, Elaine. *Rachel Carson and the Environmental Movement*. New York: Children's Press, 2004.

Leonard, Tom. "Al Gore's electricity bill goes through the (insulated) roof." *The Telegraph*. June 18, 2008. Available online. URL: http://www.telegraph.co.uk/news/worldnews/northamerica/usa/2153179/Al-Gores-electricity-bill-goes-through-the-insulated-roof.html

Lovely, Erika. "Clinton and Gore talk Smart Grid." *Politico.com*. February 23, 2009. Available online. URL: http://news.yahoo.com/s/politico/20090223/pl_politico/19194_1

Maraniss, David, and Ellen Nakashima. *The Prince of Tennessee: The Rise of Al Gore.* New York: Simon & Schuster, 2000.

Mufson, Steven. "Gore Urges Fast Energy Makeover." *The Washington Post.* July 18, 2008. Available online. URL: http://www.washington post.com/wp-dyn/content/article/2008/07/17/AR2008071700244.html

Nagourney, Adam. "Gore Wins Hollywood in a Landslide." *The New York Times.* February 25, 2007. Available online. URL: http://thecaucus. blogs.nytimes.com/2007/02/25/gore-wins-hollywood-in-a-landslide/

Oreskes, Naomi and Erik M. Conway. *Merchants of Doubt.* New York: Bloomsbury Press, 2010.

"Remarks by Al Gore, Climate Change Conference." Kyoto, Japan. December 8, 1997. Available online. URL: http://web.archive.org/web/20001207090900/www.algore.com/speeches/speeches_kyoto_120897.html

Schlesinger, Arthur, Jr. "It's a Mess, But We've Been Through It Before." *Time Pacific.* November 20, 2000. Available online. URL: http://www.time.com/time/pacific/magazine/20001120/schlesinger.html

Sibley, Lisa. "Al Gore: Super grid is critical to combating the climate crisis." *Cleantech.* November 20, 2009. Available online. URL: http://cleantech.com/news/5331/al-gore-super-grid-critical-combati

Smith, Lewis. "Al Gore's inconvenient judgment." *Times Online.* October 11, 2007. Available online. URL: http://business.timesonline.co.uk/tol/business/law/article2633838.ece

Usborne, David. "Al Gore denies he is 'carbon billionaire.'" *The Independent.* November 4, 2009. Available online. URL: http://www.independent.co.uk/environment/climate-change/al-gore-denies-he-is-carbon-billionaire-1814199.html

"Vice President Gore: Strong Environmental Leadership for the New Millennium." The White House Archives. Available online. URL: http://clinton5.nara.gov/WH/EOP/OVP/initiatives/environment.html

"Will Al's Oscar Bounce Put Him in the Race?" ABC News/Entertainment. February 26, 2007. Available online. URL: http://abcnews.go.ecom/Entertainment/story?id=2903909

Zelnick, Bob. *Gore: A Political Life.* Washington, D.C.: Regency Publishing, 1999.

Further Resources

Anderson, Dale. *Al Gore: A Wake-Up Call to Global Warming.* New York: Crabtree Publishing Company, 2009.

Gore, Al. *An Inconvenient Truth: The Crisis of Global Warming.* New York: Viking, 2007.

Gore, Al. *Earth in the Balance: Ecology and the Human Spirit.* Pennsylvania: Rodale, 2006.

Gore, Al. *Our Choice: A Plan to Solve the Climate Crisis.* Pennsylvania: Rodale, 2009.

Harmon, Daniel E. *Al Gore and Global Warming.* New York: Rosen Publishing, 2009.

McGowan, Joe. *Al Gore.* Pleasantville, NY: Gareth Stevens Publishing, 2010.

Oreskes, Naomi and Conway, Erik M. *Merchants of Doubt: How a Handful of Scientists Obscured the Truth on Issues from Tobacco Smoke to Global Warming.* New York: Bloomsbury Press, 2010.

Stefoff, Rebecca. *Al Gore.* Minneapolis: Learner Publications, 2009.

WEB SITES

Al Gore

http://www.algore.com

This is Al Gore's official Web site. It has information about the projects that he is involved in, as well as his books. A news feed provided by Environmental Health News keeps visitors up to date on any news that affects climate change.

An Inconvenient Truth

http://www.climatecrisis.net

This is the official site for Gore's documentary *An Inconvenient Truth.* The site gives more information about the film, including the changes people have made to become more climate conscious since the film was released. It also includes information about the documentary *Climate of Change,* which shows how regular people are fighting global warming.

Climate Prediction
http://climateprediction.net
This is a distributed computing project. People can sign up to allow Climate Prediction to use time on their computer to make climate predictions. The more computers they are able to use, the better their accuracy. The goal is to make climate predictions for the next 100 years. Scientists hope to see if the current climate models are correct.

Global Warming
http://globalwarmingkids.net
This site is aimed at kids who are interested in learning more about climate change. There are several groups, including Inconvenient Youth, for kids ages 13–18 to connect and talk about joining together to solve the climate crisis.

Tiki the Penguin
http://tiki.oneworld.net/global_warming/climate_home.html
The home page of Tiki the Penguin is a site for kids about things happening around the world. On the Hot Earth page, kids can learn what global warming is and what causes it, as well as what they can do to help. The site includes links to other Web pages that deal with climate change.

Picture Credits

Index

About the Author

TRACEY BAPTISTE is the author of the young adult novel *Angel's Grace,* which was named one of the 100 Best Books for Reading and Sharing in 2005 by New York City librarians. Baptiste has also written several nonfiction books, including biographies of Jerry Spinelli, Madeleine L'Engle, and Stephenie Meyer. She earned a B.A. in English Literature and an M.A. in Elementary Education from New York University, after which she was an elementary school teacher for several years. She notes that she loves everything in nature except for mosquitoes and birds that poop on her Prius. You can find out more about her at www.traceybaptiste.com.